MARK BRANDON READ

CHOPPER 10

MARK BRANDON READ

CHOPPER 10

A FOOL AND HIS TOES
ARE SOON PARTED

JOHN BLAKE

Published by John Blake Publishing Ltd,
3 Bramber Court, 2 Bramber Road,
London W14 9PB, England

www.johnblakepublishing.co.uk

First published in paperback in 2010

ISBN: 978 1 84454 912 2

British Library Cataloguing-in-Publication Data:

A catalogue record for this book is available from the British Library.

Design by www.envydesign.co.uk

Printed in Great Britain by CPI Bookmarque, Croydon

1 3 5 7 9 10 8 6 4 2

Papers used by John Blake Publishing are natural, recyclable products made
from wood grown in sustainable forests. The manufacturing processes conform
to the environmental regulations of the country of origin.

Every attempt has been made to contact the relevant copyright-holders,
but some were unobtainable. We would be grateful if the appropriate people
could contact us.

'*I have sat quietly beside the river of life and seen the bodies of all my enemies drift by...*'

MARK BRANDON READ

For all my creditors

CONTENTS

CHAPTER 1

OUTLIVING ENEMIES

I was the one voted most likely to die

What a shock to see Eagles player Ben Cousins flattened by his drug problem. For years, I have known that he and a few of his mates were hanging around some pretty well-known drug dealers in Perth. No one told them that when you lie down with drug dealers you wake up in a police cell – or a drug clinic.

Cousins thought these blokes were his friends. A drug dealer a friend? Do me a favour. It makes as much sense as keeping a scorpion as a pet.

Drug dealers are like everyone else. They love to be around famous people so they go out of their way to link up with actors, TV types and footy players.

You want the flash car, the blonde girlfriend with plastic tits and the footy-player mates. Then, in Australia, you've made it.

Now a kid like Cousins was probably given his drugs cheap to begin with but then they said he was spending $3000 a week on drugs. That's a lot of money. Where were his friends then?

The Mr Big in WA is an old Melbourne boy. With one phone call he could have told the rest of his crew, 'No more drugs for Ben.'

But he didn't. Some friend.

I like to be around famous people too. I have pictures of me with people like Jimmy Barnes, and he is a top bloke. But I am a retired crook and can't get people into trouble. If I saw Eddie McGuire in the street now, I'd go over and say hello, whereas when I was up and about I wouldn't bother him because it could cause embarrassment for him. But the Perth crew hung on to those footy players like they were the royal family and no one over there did a thing.

The police tipped off the footy club that they were going down the wrong track and what did they do?

Sweet fuck-all.

I reckon footy clubs should each have an old copper on staff. Someone like Brian 'The Skull' Murphy could be there in the background just watching what was going on and moving the wrong types out the door. Footy coaches might know a bit about the game but they don't know much else. When they told Ben to go out and get the pill, they didn't know he would take them literally.

There have been some footy players who have crossed over to the dark side. There was one famous one who was the heavy for a drug crew, though I suspect if it had got real nasty he would have headed to the interchange bench quick smart in case he got his head knocked off by the even heavier guys. If you catch my drift.

There was another player who did a good line in taking his mates' golf clubs to the pawnbroker so he could fund his gambling habits and another who moved a fair bit of counterfeit money. Just as well, he wasn't much of a ruckman and played most of his time away from the big league.

I think one of the things that made me turn into a crook was that there wasn't a war for me and I always wanted to be a soldier.

Once I went down my track, I always wanted to be the best and most famous. I knew they would remember me, Squizzy Taylor and Ned Kelly. Blokes like Alphonse were always only going to be footnotes in the history of crime.

I will always be remembered but being recognised has its down side. Most people are really nice and polite but some people are quite rude. They stuff something in front of you and say, 'Sign this.' I have always thought it should be legal to shoot maybe every tenth autograph hunter so the others will queue up politely and remember to say 'thank you'. But then again, I'm old-fashioned.

I was in the outback once when an Aboriginal boy asked for an autograph. I signed my name and he gave it back saying, 'No – use your real name – Eric Bana.' So I signed it 'Eric Bana'. Stuff it, why not? I gave him his start, and has he ever even bothered to invite Margaret and me to Hollywood?

Not even once, so bugger him. Then again, my passport might set off a few alarms at the LA airport, so maybe it doesn't matter too much, Eric.

The truth is I wasn't much of a crook: because, when you look at it, I spent more than twenty years in jail. Wasted the best years of my life. I was tough, mad and violent but the best crooks these days go to work with a pen and a computer, not with iron bars and guns.

Some blokes seem to run the underworld when they get others to do their dirty work. The real tough men are assigned to be foot soldiers. I'm glad I'm well out of it.

So I've ended up now with a few books, some paintings, a film made about me, no ears and a crook liver.

Maybe I should have been a bank clerk and worn a cardigan rather than a bulletproof jacket.

The funny thing is, in the world of crime, I was a master strategist and tactician. I was a survivor who knew the moves of my opponents and could ambush them at will.

But in the world of 'honest' business I have been constantly betrayed. When Jimmy Loughnan attacked me from behind in Pentridge I blamed myself, as I should have seen it coming. But on the outside there is no warning.

The snakes wear designer suits and the hyenas have cosmetically enhanced designer white teeth. So many people have come to me with schemes where 'we' will get rich. I didn't know that in the business world 'we' means 'they'.

There are crooks who would give you their word and that was always enough. But in the business world people lie and cheat and then go home to a roast dinner without a moment's thought.

Are they crazy? Here is me, a self-declared killer, a no-eared psychopath with a short attention span and they turn up saying, 'Look, Chopper, we're sorry but that money we promised you hasn't come through – but let's do lunch. I'll get my people to talk to your people.'

It is at moments like those I think of ringing some of my people – people like Dave the Jew or Amos Atkinson and suggest we do one more job for old time's sake.

But I have sworn that I am retired and, if the snakes want to slither around with forked tongues, what am I to do but cop it?

I am bankrupt. I owe money. My health is rooted.

For years in H Division more than thirty of us had to share the same razor when we shaved. Now all of us have hepatitis. And no one gives a stuff. Fair enough, too. We did the crimes and got locked up for what we did. No point whining about it now.

But there is one thing I do know. I promised to outlive my enemies – and now they are all dead and gone.

Bye-bye, Dennis Allen, you drug-dealing wombat. Toodleoo, Jason, Mark and Lewis Moran – the clan with big mouths and long pockets. Ciao, Alphonse, the Plastic Godfather. And see ya, Sid Collins.

I was the one voted most likely to die. But I'm still here after all these years, boxing on and still not pleading guilty.

The last man standing.

CHAPTER 2

UNDERWORLD KILLINGS

I was always a prophet for profit

In 2003, police were finally forced to admit Melbourne was in the middle of an underworld war. They responded by setting up the special gangland taskforce codenamed Purana.

The investigators quickly established that a small gang of crooks controlled by a chubby western suburban drug trafficker called Carl Williams was determined to kill most of Melbourne's established crime figures. Many of the victims could be linked to Read's old enemies – Alphonse Gangitano and the notorious Moran family.

The feud began when standover men Jason and Mark Moran shot Williams in the stomach in October 1999. Williams vowed revenge and effectively declared open season on his enemies. (At the time of writing he has been sentenced to 35 years' jail for master-

minding the audacious series of murders that came to be called the underworld war.)

But four years before police set up their taskforce, poacher-turned-gamekeeper Mark Brandon Read warned that Melbourne was about to witness a serious underworld war and predicted many of the dead and wounded would be old associates of the man he dubbed 'Fat Al'. Read was amazed that no one seemed to realise what was happening in front of their eyes.

In 1999, Read wrote:

Make no mistake, the bodies will keep falling but for reasons I don't understand no one seems to get excited. You can find it between the fashion pages and the sports lift-out. They write more about a new risotto recipe than the blood and guts of an underworld war. God help us and pass me a café latte…

Let's make it clear on the long-range forecast. Before this is finished, it will make the old Market Murders back in the Sixties look like nude mud wrestling. There is a group of whackers who ran around flogging, belting and shooting people when they were part of Al's team. Each and every one of them has been noted and their dance cards have been marked. They will all get a visit and then will head to the morgue.

In years to come, we will talk of the sabre-toothed tiger, the dodo and Alphonse's crew in the same breath… all extinct.

I was considering retiring from crime writing but from what I have heard I may have a lot more to write about quite soon. Watch this space. There are more bodies to come.

If you sit by a river for long enough, you will see the bodies of all your enemies float by.

I said that years ago.

I forgot to mention that they will float past a damn sight quicker if you have a couple of mates upstream pushing the bastards in for you.

Years before Purana was established Read predicted that a new group of criminals planned to wipe out the existing underworld power brokers. He wrote:

The media will gobble it up as an underworld war. They will never know it is an extermination programme. With any luck, some of those on the list will blame others on the list for some of the deaths and start to kill each other.

Read now gives an insider's view of the murders that fascinated Australia.

GREGORY JOHN WORKMAN

Shot dead by fellow standover man, Al Gangitano
in St Kilda on 7 February 1995

Greg wasn't a bad bloke. He came from a tough working-class family in Preston, not that he ever did much work himself. Good looking and with the gift of the gab, in the underworld sea he was neither a bottom dweller nor a shark. He was big enough to eat little fish but had to keep away from the big ones.

If he had stayed in the second division, he could have made a bit of money, done a bit of jail, given it all up, got a job, drank beer and eaten hamburgers, dying fat and happy in his mid-sixties from heart disease.

Instead, he dreamed he could be a player in the big league. But, sadly, he wasn't up to it. He was a flathead who thought he was a killer shark.

He had a falling out with Fat Al when they both ended up at a party in St Kilda. It was supposed to a be a party – a 'pull up' where everyone tipped in for bail money for a sucker who had just been snipped for some armed robberies. But Al wasn't in one of his more charitable moods and things turned nasty. Workman and Al exchanged words – they must have been loud ones because someone called the local police over the noise. The coppers were assured there wouldn't be a problem and believed them and cleared off.

I don't know what they teach them in the Academy these days. There must have been about sixty people in a room, most covered with tatts, carrying guns and drinking bourbon and the uniformed locals thought it was some kind of peace rally.

After the coppers left, Greg made the mistake of going outside with Gangitano. Maybe he thought they were going to settle matters like gentlemen. Er, I don't think so.

Al pulled out a little shooter and put eight slugs into Workman – a shocking waste of bullets and total overkill, I think.

Two sisters saw it and became police witnesses, but eventually Al reached out to them and the girls were soon flying out of the country on the holiday of a lifetime. They were soon waltzing around Disneyland, and if the homicide squad thought they had enough to bin Al they were in Fantasyland. The case collapsed and, like the police, I was saddened when he walked away.

Alphonse had been making noises about me while I was inside and I was looking forward to having a chat with him in H Division. Without his team of would-be Mafia goombahs, Al would have soon realised he was no Mr Big. A good cut-throat razor will do that. I also knew we would never square up on the outside because it was the beginning of the end for Big Al. I knew back then that Al was already on borrowed time as well as borrowed money.

After Al beat the Workman blister, his lawyer hit the coppers with nearly $70,000 in legal bills. Not everyone knows there is only one thing coppers hate more than losing and that is parting with folding notes. As they say, there are only two things that don't pay – crime and detectives.

Everywhere Al went from then on, he brought police attention and that was bad for business. He loved the idea of playing the public role of a gangster but he could see the final curtain was about to fall.

Al was a dead man walking – or, in his case, waddling. He may as well have shot himself in the head the night he shot Workman and saved someone else the trouble a few years later.

GEORGE MARCUS

A crime figure with legal connections; he was shot dead after visiting a criminal's wife in Box Hill North on 20 April 1997

Another wannabe crook disliked in some legal circles. Who killed him? Let's just say, by George, that he fought the law and the law won. The killer will never be charged.

MOTIVE: Possible underworld hit.

ALPHONSE JOHN GANGITANO

Shot dead in his Templestowe home on 16 January 1998

The beauty of being a known killer and an alleged author is that you can have an opinion on any murder and people don't know if it is a theory based on experience or the facts based on inside knowledge. Sometimes I don't know myself. I prefer not to. It's less complicated.

Take poor Alphonse. Some pretty young television thing wanted me to debate him when I got out of jail. I told the little vixen that it was not to be unless it was done through a Ouija board, as Al was about to cop a couple of lead injections in his cranium.

As suspected, Alphonse ran out of breath rather suddenly just a few weeks later.

Was that inside knowledge or just a lucky guess? Any fool could see that Alphonse was running red-hot and couldn't be allowed to keep going. But then again, I'm no fool.

Whether I had inside knowledge or just suspected what

was going to happen doesn't matter. He is dead and I am not. I can't be blamed, as I was inside Risdon Prison in cold old Tassie, well out of harm's way.

There was no way out for Fat Al. He hated me but he didn't know that I almost saved his life. He was so frightened of me that he pissed off to live in Italy for a year when I got out of prison. When I ended up back in a tin-pot prison in Tassie, he got out his double-breasted pinstripe and jumped on a Jumbo to get back to Lygon Street. If he'd stayed in Italy, he would have grown old and fat on home-made spaghetti but the trouble with Al was that he couldn't resist a walk-on part in Melbourne's gangster movie.

After he knocked Workman, he was a marked man with the coppers and he brought attention to everyone. He had to go. It was said that his pal Jason Moran pulled the trigger on him.

It is so often the case in underworld killings. If a man who fires the bullet is not a friend, the person who sent him there often is.

Jason was supposed to have gone to Al's that night for a chat with the rule that there would be no guns but Jason cheated, pulled out the shooter and that was it. Good friend 'The Munster' Graham Kinniburgh was there too but he was almost as shocked as Big Al when the bullets started flying. Kinniburgh was a seriously good crook who flew under the radar for years. Why he got connected with Alphonse I will never know, but it would prove to be a fatal misjudgement in the end.

Jason always said he didn't do it but I beg to differ. What I don't know is whether he went there to do it. I would suspect not. He was always just a dickhead who pulled guns when he lost an argument. He would have been knocked years earlier except his family had pull with many heavies back then and he was allowed to put holes in his manners when someone should have put a hole in his guts as a lesson.

I believe he lost his temper that night and just started shooting.

Kinniburgh did a runner after the shooting and probably would never have been linked to the whole mess, but after he left he saw Alphonse's missus and kids driving down the street. At least he drove back so they wouldn't have to deal with the whole mess on their own. The Munster showed a bit of dash that night. He ended up linked to the crime and his low profile was fucked then and there.

In his paranoid world, Alphonse always thought I would be the one who would come after him but I knew it would be his friends, not his enemies who would knock Al from his perch.

Alphonse was always a salesman at heart. Sharp, well dressed, well spoken, fairly well educated from a fairly well-to-do family, but a fucking salesman. That's all. He sold shit and told people it was chocolate.

The Mafia began as a group of honourable men who fought for the poor and then it got corrupted into a crime gang. Then idiots like Alphonse tried to jump on board wearing imported clothes, eating garlic and kissing people on the cheeks, and sometimes on the face too.

Eventually, the fiction becomes a reality but Alphonse didn't flick to the end of the book of his own life of make-believe. It ended with him being shot. Everyone knew what was on the last page but the poor fat slob himself. His fantasy became reality and he ended up dead. I guess this book, if you bother to read further, is meant to help the reader unravel the sticky mess of glue that holds the legend together.

If Alphonse had known what was going to happen, would he have lived his life differently? I wonder. I suspect not. He got his picture in the paper.

Some people who believed the crap actually treated him with respect. If it weren't for the myth, he would have been just another used-car salesman in a bad suit.

This is what I wrote about him eight years before he popped off. Was I right? You be the judge.

'Another major figure we will call Al is Lygon Street's answer to Robert De Niro. He goes under many names: The Fairy Godfather, The Plastic Gangster, Melbourne's Princess of Crime, the King of Paranoia and the Italian French Poodle. That's right, I don't like Al. I first met him when he was 19, pinching money out of girls' handbags in nightclubs while the chicks were on the dance floor.

'I've never heard of Al having a punch-on without having ten or twelve helpers backing him up. He is a bully and he picks his mark. He will only fight if he can win. He started off as a bouncer at the two-up school; he has shot a few drunks in the leg at nightclubs and he has learned how to run card games. He may be rich and he may be well connected but the hole he will one day go into has already been dug.

'He lives in fear, a prisoner of his own wealth. He is backed up by a private army of kick boxers, gunmen and bouncers, all with their hands out for money. The only one in that crew with guts and brains is the one called Mick [Gatto], who has a sense not to shoot his mouth off.

'Every time Al needs some advice he puts on *The Godfather* movie to see how Marlon Brando did it. Once I went to say a friendly hello to him in a card game in Lygon Street – with a stick of gelignite. Funny thing, Al wouldn't come out of the toilets for a chat.

'This big clown may be a hero to a large part of the criminal world but personally I wouldn't give him a job as a towel boy in a gay Turkish bath: he wouldn't be tough enough. He is another of that crew who is that master of the swap-out, which is why he hasn't been to jail.'

You see? I was always a prophet for profit.

JOHN FURLAN

Died when his white Subaru Liberty exploded as he drove it along Lorenson Avenue, Merlynston, on 3 August 1998

Johnny Furlan was another 'businessman' who thought he was a tough guy. He was wrong. He had a dispute with a spivvy used-car salesman named Mick. Trouble was Mick wasn't an Irish

Mick who would settle any blues over twenty pints of Guinness and a punch-on but a woggy one called Domenico Italiano.

Italiano liked to think of himself as connected. His granddad was Domenico Italiano, who was Victoria's undisputed Mafia Godfather in the 1950s. When the old man died from natural causes all the would-be Mafia Dons got excited and that resulted in the Melbourne market murders of 1963–64.

Anyway, young Dom and Furlan had a blue over a number of things. At one stage, Dom rented a car yard from Furlan in Sydney Road and when it went guts up Johnny still wanted his money.

Furlan was looking to sell out of his businesses and move to Tassie to go fishing and that should have been the end of it.

Trouble was, Italiano may have been as fat as an elephant but he had a memory like one too. For whatever reason, Italiano hired a young bloke to plonk a bomb in Furlan's car and they blew him up. It was such a big blast they probably saved him the airfare back to Tassie.

Johnny used to sell pretty dodgy cars. He sold bombs, then he died in one. There was a little bit of poetry there.

Big Fat Mick was never charged over the bomb. The young fellow was about to tip a bucket on him when he mysteriously committed suicide.

Italiano went to jail for fraud, won a retrial and was really excited when he got out of jail in 2005. Too excited, as it turned out. He went and bought some Viagra to get rid of some pent-up frustration with an old girlfriend the next day.

It was too much for his ticker and he died on the nest, which happens more often than a lot of people reckon. Talk about a hard case to crack. All that time behind bars and then he died with one in his undies.

He bombed out on both counts, Ha ha.

MAD CHARLIE HEGYALJI

Shot dead in the front garden of his South Caulfield home on 23 November 1998

The murder of Mad Charlie was for me a great personal sadness. I even named my first son after him. He was, in spite of fallouts from the past, an old and dear friend. But, in my old line of work, friendships can be fatal.

A friend, a man who didn't want to kill him but could see no other way out of this particular problem, killed Charlie.

Charlie had always said, 'When my time comes, let it not be at the hands of a laughing enemy but at the hands of a crying friend.' He got his wish. I can tell Charlie that the tears over what had to be done were flowing before his death and are still flowing.

It was a classic ambush. The killer lay in wait – literally. He hid under the bushes in the front yard, waited until Charlie came home that night and that was it.

I think Charlie knew it was coming. He rang me when I was still living in Tassie for a chat days before he was shot. It was like talking to a dead man. I knew he was gone and I think he did too.

The truth was Charlie had lost his army. When the barman calls last drinks, you leave. Charlie refused to leave. He was all alone and feeling a bit sorry for himself. I felt a bit sad for Charlie myself after hearing all of that, but what could I do? Go back to Melbourne and hold his hand?

If I had done that, I knew we would both die. I would bring trouble to him, not protect him from it. I'd held Charlie's hand for many years – for far too many years, some might say – and now it was up to Charlie to face his own demons all on his own. In the 1980s, Charlie was a powerful man but only because of those who stood next to him.

Mad Charlie had the power of life and death because his crew was made up of psychopaths pretending to be business-men, not businessmen pretending to be nutters.

In the classic *Chopper from the Inside*, I wrote, 'Charlie studied Mafia crime books like a priest studied the Bible. In late 1989, he was shot in the guts in front of his $250,000 South Caulfield home.

'He's still alive, but his dreams of underworld glory never reached his teenage fantasies. All he has now are his Mafia books and his collection of gangster videos. But to the underworld kingpins who might laugh at Charlie now… in 1974 one word from him could have seen them all dead, and changed the face of the underworld forever. We had the death list, the guns and the insanity to carry it out.'

However, by the late 1990s Charlie was a general with-out an army. I felt sorry for him, but Charlie always forgot that it was other people who put him where he was and when those certain few people walked away from him he was finished.

What happened had to happen. I'm surprised it took so long.

From this distance it was like watching a car crash in slow motion.

Goodbye, Charlie – I still miss you.

Mad Charlie was very rich when he died, but no one seems to have worked out what happened to his money. Funny, that.

VINCE MANNELLA

Shot as he returned to his North Fitzroy
home on 9 January 1999

I'll tell you who killed poor old Hollywood Vince. They should charge Quentin Tarantino and the rest of the movie moguls who pump up the Mafia. I reckon clowns like Vince think gangster flicks are documentaries and not make-believe.

No one would ever have heard of Vince if he hadn't made the papers by having his brains splattered over his own welcome mat. In the underworld he was a doorman who ended up thinking he owned the hotel. The truth is he was just another deluded dago who lived on the scraps thrown from Alphonse's table.

Way back in the Seventies, Vince was a regular around the gambling joints in Carlton but the would-be wise guy was always wise enough to look the other way when I popped in for some walk-around money.

He used to carry knives and guns back then but he knew that, when he put his hands in his pockets around me back then, it was only to pull cash out as a gesture of friendship.

Vince was a man with a reputation for being able to get anything, from amphetamine chemicals for a cook to truckloads of food or stolen cigarettes. He was like an olive-oil version of Arthur Daley.

He shot some poor wog seven times when he was banned from playing cards in a coffee shop in Carlton. The bloke survived and Vinnie got about seven years. That's one year per shot, which is about the going rate.

When he got out, he thought he was some Mafia hood. If he had just stuck to being a good honest thief, he might be still with us but with Alphonse gone he thought he could move from being a waiter to sitting at the head of the table.

Too arrogant to know his limitations and too dumb to see it coming, he didn't know he was a member of an endangered species: Melbourne wogs who want to be mobsters.

He was a bit of a night owl, but killers know if they wait in the bushes at the victim's home it will never be a matter of if, just when.

When they found him his head was on the welcome mat. At least it kept the blood off the imported Italian tiles. They can be buggers to clean. I know.

JOE QUADARA

Shot dead as he arrived at work at a Toorak supermarket
at 3am on 28 May 1999

Joe was as regular as clockwork and that made him an easy target when his time came. He pulled up as he always did outside the supermarket where he worked and they were waiting. It was clean as a whistle. Joe was once a rich greengrocer who had owned his own shops but he went belly up. He owed people money and they were sick of waiting. What nobody knew was that he had cancer and was dying anyway. The killers just hurried the process up a bit.

Joe might have known the price of grapefruit but he didn't know much about gangsters.

Notice how many people connected with the fruit and vegetable industry end up getting murdered? I reckon all vegetarians are closet homicidal maniacs. No one kills butchers, do they? Funny, that.

VICKI JACOBS

Shot dead as she slept with her six-year-old son in the
Bendigo suburb of Long Gully on 12 June 1999

How a nice kid like Vicki Jacobs got dragged into this is a disgrace. Now, I've done plenty of things I now regret. Like shooting one guy in the leg. He didn't deserve it. And not shooting Nick Apostolidis in the head. He did.

Most underworld killings are a case of right whack. Men

who choose to make a living through violence can hardly complain when they become victims. Of course, they can't because they are dead. Who wants to listen to a dead bloke complaining that he is stiff?

If I had copped it before I retired, then so be it.

Underworld killings are usually just good sport, but every now and again the line is crossed. Vicki Jacobs was a girl who had cleaned up her act. To kill her was an act of cowardly revenge for no good purpose.

Sure, she had run with the wrong crowd but she had built a new life – until someone took it from her.

She knew bikies and dabbled in drugs and her husband was into everything he could find.

She had the brains to split from him but Gerald Preston just kept on trying to be a tough guy. He went over to Adelaide to kill a couple of blokes for the bikies but didn't have the brains to plan it properly and it was just a matter of time before he got snipped. He got paid $10,000 to do the job and, as you know, if you pay peanuts you end up with a hairy chimp rather than a professional hitman.

He ended up getting 32 years after Vicki gave evidence against him. He blamed her for his predicament when he should have blamed those who got him to do the job in the first place.

She was offered police protection but she thought she could disappear to go to Bendigo with her young son and leave the underworld forever. While Preston was in jail his hatred fermented. I can tell you that, from inside jail, it is easy to reach out and touch someone. There is no doubt someone did him a favour. Almost certainly it would be the bloke who got him to do the double whack in Adelaide. That bloke is a Hells Angel who was out of the country at the time. Must have got someone else to do the dirty work again. Vicki was asleep with her son when someone just blew her away.

Preston even had the gall to put a death notice in the paper that said, 'Soulmates once, you gave us a beautiful healthy son and blossomed as a proud, devoted mother. Truly. And while we grew apart I always admired your strength and never stopped missing you… You will always be in our hearts.'

That's Gerald Preston: a louse, a hypocrite and a tosser. It's enough to give killers a bad reputation.

There is still a million-dollar reward for anyone who can help solve the murder. I'll do it for nothing.

They may never prove it but a man connected with the Angels came down from Darwin to Adelaide, then jumped in a hire car and drove to Melbourne.

A local bikie drove the killer up to Bendigo and the job was done. It was on the night that Melbourne Angels had a big party so they could all alibi each other.

Funny, that. I can understand if they had killed her before she gave evidence as it could have stuffed the case. But after? Just cold-blooded revenge. She couldn't hurt them any more but they just wanted her dead as a warning to others.

But justice works in mysterious ways. Preston lost his appeal and will rot in jail until he is an old man.

As for the bloke who organised it on the outside, he has

had a big falling out with his old bikie crew and has been thrown out of the gang. When you leave the Hells Angels they take all your mementos. Things like your jacket, stubbie-holder and belt buckle have to be returned so you can't sell them on eBay. But what about the Hells Angels tatts? Sorry, they have to go too. So do you think they would hire a gentle plastic surgeon with a light touch in laser surgery?

Well, the Angels may be many things but they are not New Age Fairies. No, they do it the old-fashioned way. The tatts were removed with an angle grinder and a steam iron.

No wonder he was permanently de-pressed. Ha, Ha.

DIMITRIOS BELIAS

Found by cleaners in a pool of blood below a
St Kilda Road office on 9 September 1999

Goodbye, Jimmy the Greek, a small-time bit player in a much larger production. Dimitrios Belias, thirty-eight years old, got it on 9/9/99 in the car park of a St Kilda Road office complex. Interesting date, good postcode, bad head wound.

Mad Charlie called Jimmy the Greek his money mover. He acted as a front man in card games, using Mad Charlie's money, many years ago. He also bought and sold property for Charlie. He also did work for Alphonse and a few others over the years. He was not a full-time full-on criminal. He would go to the edge without getting his hands dirty.

Jimmy the Greek was a small cog in an organised crime

wheel, simply part of the machine. He would not be worth a mention except for the way he died. It is just that the death of Alphonse, then Mad Charlie, has made a lot of mice turn into lions overnight. The reserves are now getting a game in the seniors and some of them won't be up to it when the going gets tough.

In the old days, Jimmy the Greek could be controlled with a backhander. The fact that he was put off indicated he had risen to a level where he was important enough to kill.

Some of the shit kickers have been promoted over the graves of their former bosses.

Jimmy would borrow money to gamble. He was a good gambler but he wasn't as good at keeping his word of honour.

When he broke his word, he may have received a slap in the mouth a few years ago from men who are now dead. Lions can afford to forgive, mice can't afford such grand gestures.

You didn't know when to fold and walk away. You kept playing and they carried you out feet first.

Bang, bang, see you later, Jimmy.

GERARDO MANNELLA

Shot dead as he left his brother's North Fitzroy
home on 20 October 1999

Killing peanuts in the underworld is a little like eating peanuts with beer: one is never enough.

Poor old Gerry wasn't a bad bloke and he would have lived a long life if his brother hadn't been a nuisance. But those who killed Vince found that Gerry was making enquiries and they decided that they were going to put a full stop on the debate.

They thought that if Gerry found out who killed his brother he might want to do something about it. He was telling people he was going to square up for his brother. It is most unwise to speak openly about these matters because if people take you seriously they will be forced to get in first. Dead men can't hurt anybody.

If you are going to do it, don't talk about it. If you're not going to do it, then definitely don't talk about it.

He was at his brother Sal's place when he saw the gunmen. He then knew the answer to the question and he also knew that he should never have asked it. He yelled out 'No!', which was an obvious waste of one of his last breaths, and then took off. He got about fifty metres, which wasn't a bad effort.

Gerry was the pacemaker but you can't outrun a bullet.

The unfortunately named Sal Mannella has been wise enough to keep his head down since. Which is a pity because some scallywags on the radio love to take poor old Sal's name in vain.

FRANK BENEVENTO

Shot dead in Beaumaris on 8 May 2000

I thought these Mafia blokes were supposed to know a bit about history. If Frank had an eye on what was happening, he might have taken early retirement rather than hanging around to take the lead redundancy package.

Frank's old man was Liborio Benvenuto, who was the Mafia

Godfather in Victoria in the good old days. The old man was polite and charming. He could always afford to be nice because few people wanted to see him turn nasty. Someone blew up his car outside the market in the 1980s and a short time later two blokes ended up at the bottom of the Murrumbidgee River minus a few working parts.

But, after Liborio died, Frank could never step up to take his place.

He didn't have that much when he died but he did own $5000 worth of racing pigeons. Perhaps he should have been more interested in the other type – stool pigeons. Because someone gave him up big time. Benji Veniamin shot him, but instead of pissing off straight away Benji should have looked in the boot of the car. There was more than $60,000 in old notes stashed in it. Ha ha, Benji.

Frank managed to press the speed dial on his phone to ring his mate Victor Peirce after he was shot but it was already too late. It wouldn't have mattered if he had rung Christian Barnard. It was already all over.

If he had been able to say anything, it might have been 'Benji' or he might have said 'Mark Moran' who I have been told might have been taking in the sea air at Beaumaris around that time.

Victor later had a meeting with Benji to show there were no hard feelings and business was business. Didn't do anyone any good as Benji, Victor and Mark all ended up very dead.

Thank goodness I am just a peaceful painter these days. That underworld shit is pretty scary.

RICHARD MLADENICH

Shot dead while visiting a friend in a St Kilda
motel unit on 16 May 2000

Read wrote of Mad Richard in 1994: 'Richard Victor Mladenich, spoke to the *Truth* newspaper a short while ago and called me unkind names.

'Poor Richard. The last time I saw him was in H Division, Pentridge. He had fallen over and hit his head rather savagely on a sharp heavy instrument and was pissing blood at a fast and furious rate of knots.

'I don't know if it was an accident or if poor Richard was the victim of terrible foul play. Nevertheless, Richard is not a man who tells on people in police stations, so if he was attacked his attacker went unpunished.

'It was rumoured that I once put the blade of a garden spade through the right side of his skull, nearly killing him in H Division at Pentridge in 1989, but Richard stuck staunch and told police nothing. The two prison officers who witnessed it told police nothing, either. That's how H Division ran back then. Ah, the good old days.

'Richard was a loud mouth who could make you laugh on a good day and make you want to bury a spade in his head on a bad one. He didn't know when to shut up.

'Richard has had a long-running battle with the needle and his personality has taken a dive as a result.

'For the life of me I don't understand why he dislikes me so much. That accidental tap on the skull must have affected his state of mind and I am shocked and somewhat hurt that he could express any sort of ill-will towards me.

'I will mention the dear boy in my prayers. Ha ha.'

After one of his many stints in jail Richard tried to become a big player in the drug world but he lacked the back-up. He aligned himself with Mark Moran and was a sort of minder. It wasn't the first time that Richard backed the wrong horse. He was killed by another one of those nuts from the western suburbs, Dino Dibra. Mark Moran was shot about a month later. Richard got his because he was seen as a solider for the Morans and the soldier always gets one in the head before the generals.

Richard was better at stand-up than standover. His killer knew where he was on the night he got it. Another one set up by a friend.

MARK MORAN

Shot dead outside his luxury home near
Essendon on 15 June 2000

Revenge is a dish best served cold and Mark was a marked man who was shot in cold blood over an old feud. Mark was a good-looking bloke with not a bad brain and I always felt he might have had a chance if he hadn't been brought up in the world of crime.

His dad, another popgun gangster, Leslie John Cole, was ambushed and shot dead outside his Sydney home on 10 November 1982.

Now you can't help who your dad is, but Mark never had a chance to start over because his dear old mummy, Judy, had already moved on to Lewis Moran.

So, for Mark, it was a case of moving from the criminal version of the Beverly Hillbillies to the Griswalds – I'm talking about the Morons – sorry, I mean the Morans. His half-brother was Jason – another half-wit with a De Niro complex.

Mark hadn't worked for years and lived in a house worth over $1 million. Who says crime doesn't pay?

He was one of the young gangsters, into pop and pill-pushing. He was a major drug trafficker who liked to carry a gun with a laser sight. Might have helped him if was attacked by Martians but not much good when he was ambushed by a fat drug dealer with an axe to grind and a shotgun to back it up.

He was another one who must have been set up by a friend. He left his house late at night and when he returned the killer was waiting. That killer was Carl Williams and he had been there only ten minutes. His timing was impeccable. I suspected he was tipped off and knew exactly when the soon-to-be corpse would be back.

Mark had been with Jason when Jason shot Carl in the guts in a park eight months earlier. Mark told tough-guy Jason to shoot him in the head but Jason thought he knew better. He thought if he shot Carl with a dum-dum in the tum-tum Fatty Williams would fall into line. But Carl wanted revenge and Mark was one of those who didn't know the clock was ticking. There are two things you can't help:

bad luck and a bullet in the brain. Sometimes you get both at once.

DINO DIBRA

Dibra was shot dead outside his Krambruk Street, West Sunshine, home on 14 October 2000

When Dino Dibra starts getting spoken of as a heavy hitter, we are all in deep trouble. A street punk with a shooter, he actually thought he was on the way up when he was on the way out. Criminal soldiers who think they will be generals are a penny a truckload. They end up in a cemetery or a prison cell.

What is it about the young gangsters of today? When I decided to take on the underworld, I studied the great generals. I read the *Art of War*, I read history and I talked to old soldiers. I developed strategies, and I studied my enemies like a scientist studies specimens. I knew their strengths and weakness and I would know what they were thinking before they even thought it. Then I recruited a handpicked squad of dangerous lunatics who would fight to the death for me.

Today numb-nuts like Dibra think snorting speed and carrying a gun makes you a tough guy. He was a shocking driver, too. He was once put in jail and ordered off the road for five years.

In the criminal world, he was not considered a deep thinker. He tried kidnapping but that wasn't his go either. Now even Mr and Mrs Average would know if you wanted to kidnap someone you'd do it at night and pick somewhere people were not likely to notice you. But Dummy Dibra thought he knew better and grabbed a bloke off the street and put him in the boot in front of half the world.

Then he drove off like some woggy tough guy with the doof-doof music blaring. Trouble was the bloke flicked the boot latch at the lights and jumped out and ran off. Dino and his team chased him, flogged him and chucked him back in the boot – in broad daylight in a Melbourne street in front of witnesses. Not the act of a master criminal.

Police also had his house bugged so when he rang his victim's brother to demand a ransom police recorded the lot. They also found some more evidence that was pretty handy... when they got there, the bloke was still in the boot.

It's enough to make you cry. Dino and his mate once pulled some innocent punter over after a minor traffic problem and pumped five bullets into him. A bit of overkill if you ask me.

Dibra probably was there when Mad Richard got shot in St Kilda, so he thought he was a gunman on the make. But it wasn't long before Dino copped his whack, care of his old mates Paul Kallipolitis and Benji Veniamin. If Dino had read *Chopper*, he would have known that most hits are carried out by your mates. Too late, now. If you lie down with dogs, you get up with fleas. If you lay down with Benji, you didn't get up at all.

GEORGE GERMANOS

Repeatedly shot in an Armadale park on 22 March 2001

Big George was fast with his fists and slow with his brain. A bouncer with no neck, he had been one of those power lifters who thought steroids and bench presses make you a tough guy. He tried to prove it by beating up young bucks full of bad manners and bourbon and coke. George didn't seem to know that you've got to bash someone of substance to build a reputation.

He also couldn't work out that you just have to be strong enough to pick up a .38 revolver to put a hole in the biggest chests around.

He worked in pubs, sold some gear, bashed a few customers and then moved on. He never learned the saying that you should pick on your own size.

Rumour has it that Big George finally flogged the wrong man out the back of a St Kilda nightclub. The young bloke didn't go to the police but he did talk to his dad, who was a well-known crook who didn't like his son and heir having holes punched in him by a bouncer on the make.

The crook bided his time and made a few calls. Soon a big Melbourne drug dealer made sure he became close to George. He thought he was on the road to riches when he was really standing on the pirate's plank about to take the big dive.

He was being set up but was too stupid, too greedy and too full of steroids to know it.

When the time was right, he was invited to a meeting in a park. Goofy George should have stayed home and watched TV but he went. He was never going to come back alive.

He went to a spot called Inverness Park in Armadale that was a perfect place for an ambush. There were five streets that ran into the park so the killer had a choice of which way to go in and go out. In my younger days, if I needed to meet scallywags, I would pick the spot. I would know it and I would get there early. George didn't know the joint and his street directory was open in his car on the page showing the park.

George walked in the park and copped it in the chest and then the head. He didn't know his killer but his killer knew him. He should have learned lesson one for apprentice gangsters. Never trust your friends. He should have also learned lesson two. Don't flog the son of a seriously connected gangster unless you are prepared to go all the way.

VICTOR GEORGE PEIRCE

Shot in his car in Bay Street, Port Melbourne on 1 May 2002

A classic story of a bloke addicted to crime who didn't know his number was up until he got it between the eyes.

He was the luckiest bloke alive until he wasn't. Vic helped organise the murder of two young coppers in Walsh Street, South Yarra, in 1988. A jury acquitted him but I always thought he would cop a bullet or 20 from the coppers later on (in self-defence, naturally). I was wrong about that. It was the crooks that got him in the end, not the coppers.

Walsh Street was a dog's act. Peirce and his crew thought the armed robbery squad was hunting them down and they wanted revenge. But they didn't fancy going up against the 'robbers' so the gutless wonders set some random ambush for any kid coppers they could find. *(Constables Stephen Tynan and Damien Eyre were shot dead after being lured to Walsh Street to investigate an abandoned car.)*

I'd known Vic since he was a kid. He was just 14 and starting off as a little crook when I met him. He was bright enough, but he had no chance. His half-brother was a lunatic crook named Dennis Allen. I belted Dennis within an inch of his life in B Division in Pentridge. I am not big-noting. A nun with a crook shoulder and a butterfly net could have flogged Dennis. He was not brave, just vicious. He killed many junkies with a needle and was the hotshot king of Melbourne, but when it came to standing toe to toe he would leave that for others.

His mother was Crazy Kath Pettingill. If she had had her tubes tied when she was young, there would have been half as many gunmen in Melbourne, I promise you, and the gene pool would be much improved. When she says, 'Is that a pistol in your pocket or are you just glad to see me?' I would say it was a pistol. Carrying a loaded pistol with the safety off would be safer than sticking your weapon anywhere near Kath.

Dennis spent half his waking life selling drugs, a quarter sucking up to coppers to keep out of jail and the rest of the time trying to kill me. When it came to drugs he was top rate, when it came to paying crooked cops or giving them information he was dux of the class, but when it came to trying to kill Chopper… it was like putting a three-year-old in a chess championship. He was out of his depth.

The only one of that group I had any time for was Peter Allen, who was a top jailhouse lawyer and not a bad bloke in his own way.

Vic got caught up with Dennis and the rest is history. After he and his pack of nutbag armed robbers killed those coppers in Walsh Street, Vic should have packed it in but he just loved being a crook.

When he did an armed robbery, he would get so excited he would bar up. I'm all for loving your work but that's a little over the top if you ask me. When they said he was a stick-up man, they really meant it. But when he jumped into the drugs, any sense of reality in him packed up and moved to Rio.

After his best mate Frankie Benvenuto was murdered, Vic found out the killer was little Andrew 'Benji' Veniamin.

Vic and Benji had a meeting to convince each other there would be no square up. Imagine that, such gentlemen, such men of their words. I would rather trust a cobra with a cocaine problem than one of them but that's the way they do it these days, I suppose. Meetings in parks, I'm so over them. I'd rather a weak tea in an art gallery, but, then again, I'm quite the sophisticate.

Vic apparently thought there could be some easy money to be made in the underworld war and accepted a contract to knock Jason Moran. He wanted $200,000 and took half as a down payment. But Victor wouldn't deliver the body and wasn't too keen on making a refund. The people who took the contract out were unhappy and they are the ones who decided to terminate the deal and terminate Vic at the same time.

Benji was the shooter. He must have told a little fib when he told Vic they should have a truce after the Benvenuto shooting.

Vic was shot in Bay Street, Port Melbourne, not far from his home. He was waiting for a meeting with a friend. Was he set up? Maybe someone with the same surname as his great mate Frank Benvenuto could answer that. But he won't.

Another crook, Mark Smith, got shot in the neck because he took the contract to kill Jason and then reneged. Not a good career move, I would have thought.

Funny thing is that Jason turned up at Vic's funeral. I wonder if he knew Peirce had accepted a contract to kill him. Or maybe Vic had flipped the people who set up the contract and warned Moran what was coming. Doesn't matter much. Vic's dead, Jason's dead and Benji's dead.

You would think police wouldn't try too hard to find the killers of Victor Peirce after what he did at Walsh Street but they have had a dip. They can't get the shooter unless they have an extradition treaty with the Devil but they can get the getaway driver who took Benji from the scene. That bloke's still breathing, for the moment.

Silly Kath kept saying she was going to back up for Vic. She should stick to her bingo at Venus Bay while she can. Wonder if her favourite number is still 69 like it was when she would take her teeth out for the lemon chicken when she worked in the parlours. These days the only thing she could back up is a toilet.

PAUL KALLIPOLITIS

Shot dead in his West Sunshine home.
Body found 25 October 2002

Paul Kallipolitis killed a bloke when he shot him twice in the head back in 1994. He beat the murder blue on appeal and did a little bit of time for manslaughter but didn't learn his lesson. He was another of the western suburbs crew who wanted to make the big time. Was big into speed and was a bit of kick boxer, but being fast with your feet won't stop a bullet.

He was a panel beater who preferred to beat people around the head than bother about knocking out dents from cars. As a young bloke he was making a fortune out of drugs. If he'd kept a low profile, he might have kept going but he had to have the usual toys. He had the hotted-up Holden and had the personalised plates CORRUPT attached. What? Why didn't he just get DUMB DRUG DEALER or wouldn't that fit?

One of his best friends was Andrew Veniamin but Benji was never a sentimental bloke, just a semi-mental one. He was the one who shot Paul. Whether it was orders from above or Benji was having a bad hair day, who knows? Maybe Benji just got in first – after all, business is business.

Kallipolitis was paranoid from the drugs and spent most of

his time inside his house that he fortified to protect himself from his growing list of enemies.

But as usual in the underworld you have to worry more about your friends than your enemies. Only his best mates and favourite customers were allowed into his house. So it would have been a surprise when police were called that they found the security door and the heavily bolted front door unlocked.

Not that Paul needed to worry any more about the security breach, as he was dead in his bedroom with two bullets in the brain. He usually carried his guns but this time his pistol was hidden under the mattress a couple of metres away. Not too smart unless he was expecting to be attacked by killer bed bugs.

When you are made redundant in the underworld, you well and truly get the bullet.

NIK 'THE BULGARIAN' RADEV

Shot in Queen Street, Coburg, on 15 April 2003

Nik Radev was born an idiot and went backwards from there. He arrived in Australia in the early 1980s and got a job in a fish and chip shop for about six months. Then he'd had enough of hard work and decided to get out of the fast-food industry to move into the drug business. The only chips he wanted were the $1000 variety he used at the casino.

When he got married, he came out in his going-away gear dressed like Al Pacino in *Scarface* – the white suit with the red open-necked shirt. He should have been shot on the grounds of crimes against fashion and no Australian jury would convict.

Maybe it was because Nik was an immigrant, but he always struggled with the tax system. He solved that problem by not paying a cent for 20 years. Not that it worried him. His attitude to personal accounting has always been cavalier, to say the least.

Radev could have made a fortune through his drug connections but he wanted to be the tough guy as well. He fire-bombed Willie Thompson's car over a debt of $40,000.

He stood over people and gave the impression he ran the Russian Mafia but he was just a middleweight who bummed around in and out of jail until he started selling pills around 2000.

All of a sudden, Nik was rolling in it. He bought the black Mercedes, the imported suits and French cognac. He employed his own bodyguard, using a pro kick boxer. The knucklehead didn't know that a gunman usually wins on points against a kick boxer. He wore Versace (I'm more a King Gee man myself) and had a $20,000 imported watch, which didn't tell him his time was running out.

Radev wanted to run everything. He would go into partnerships and then take over, dudding his partners.

He was allegedly connected with a group who flogged Tony Mokbel (cocaine and drug dealer who fled Australia and was recaptured in Greece in June 2007) in Lygon Street. Now Tony was about as rich as Kerry Packer, nearly as ugly and had about as long a memory as well. Tony was not a man to take a beating lying down. Well, he was, actually. He was lying down while they kicked the shit out of him.

But Radev had his eye on the amphet cook who worked for Williams and Mokbel. His plan was to get an introduction and then abduct the cook, torture him until he resigned from the Williams/Mokbel crew and decided to work for him full-time. That was workplace relations, Bulgarian style.

Now Carl and Tony didn't like the idea of losing their best man to mad Nik, so a set-up was planned.

Nik met with members of the crew at the Brighton Baths café for a latte, then they headed off to Coburg for the big introduction.

But Benji Veniamin was there, driven by one of Australia's best armed robbers. Nik arrived, hopped out of his Merc and was shot several times in the head.

The getaway car was a little Holden Vectra. Funny that Carl's dad, George, had one exactly the same. Must be a total coincidence.

The police were stuffed, even though they put out the word they would look after any insiders who were prepared to give evidence.

Or put more simply: Nik's Knocked, Paddy's Whacked, Gave the Dogs Some Bones, Carl's Old Man Went Rolling Home.

Thank you. For a few quid, you want Shakespeare?

Please pay at the door.

Nik's mates were quick to organise a wake. They headed back to his place and found $200,000 in cash – none felt the need to hand any of it over to his family. How dare they, did they think they worked for the drug squad?

He was buried in a $30,000 gold casket. Big deal – he was just another cardboard crim who thought the world was a movie and he was the star.

Nik arrived in Australia with a bad attitude and bad teeth. He couldn't fix the first but he could do something about the second. He went to a top-of-the-range dentist and said he wanted Hollywood teeth – perfect white ones that made him look like he was out of *Baywatch*. Well, sort of.

The dentist must have known Nik was in the drug business and declared it would cost $50,000. Nik didn't say a word, got up, went outside, went to the boot of the Benz and came back with the cash.

What a waste of good money. After many appointments, the dentist finally finished and the teeth were perfectly capped.

No sooner was the job finished than Nik got himself shot seven times. Sadly there's no money-back guarantee on a mouthful of lead fillings.

Look at old Chopper, still got the old false teeth but at least I'm around to use them.

Nik the Bulgarian? Bit off more than he could chew, even with flash new teeth.

SHANE CHARTRES-ABBOTT

A 28-year-old male prostitute, he was gunned down on 6 June 2003, in Howard Street, Reservoir, as he left home to defend charges in the Victorian County Court that he had raped and attacked a female client

Violent little bisexual prostitute who copped it at both ends. So it was bye-bye bi-boy. Who cares?

JASON MORAN

Shot in car park of the Cross Keys Hotel, Essendon North, on 21 June 2003

Back in 2001, I wrote this. Nostradamus could not have done it better. 'Friends of mine from Melbourne have told me to expect a new wave of murders. At least three, including at least one with a Moran influence to it.

'I will watch and wait. I see the names of some crooks in the papers. I wonder if they know they are dead men walking.

'Some of them don't know that their best friends are plotting their deaths. Have another short black, fellas. It is much later than you think.'

The Moran name was big in Melbourne crime circles for 30 years. Jason was related through marriage to the Kane standover family. On bloodlines he should have been a master criminal but he was just another big-noter with a gun and a wardrobe of imported suits.

For years, he ran around bashing and shooting any-one who looked the other way. But he always waited until he could launch a sneak attack or he had the numbers on his side. I have no problem with that. Good gangsters are like good politicians. They wait until they have the numbers before they move and they also do their best work in the dark.

When Jason was an up-and-comer, he could have been squashed but his surname meant many experienced crooks cut him some slack because of respect for his family. But he developed a bad habit of pulling his gun and then not using it. You can only bluff so many times.

Now Jason was a wannabe nutbag who used to play gangster against harmless cleanskins. He bashed one with a brick and another with a wheel brace. His dad, Lewis, never pulled him up so he ran wild.

He and Fat Al stated bashing people in a bar. They were both filled with drugs and bad movies so they thought they would get away with it. The coppers turned up and they were charged. It was the beginning of the end of a beautiful friendship.

They fell out on how they should handle their defence and we all know Jason ended up shooting his best mate.

The others started to realise that Jason couldn't be trusted. Then he shot Carl Williams in the guts and didn't have the brains to either square up with him or finish the job. He was so arrogant and so far into gangster-land he thought Williams would just roll over and take it.

But Williams backed up. Even after he had killed Jason's

half-brother Mark, Jason was still too stupid to get in first.

When Jason got out of jail, the Parole Board let him piss off overseas because everyone knew he was on a death list. If he didn't know, he just had to look at the back cover of my previous seminal works. He would have seen three grave sites on the cover. One had the name 'Big Al' and the date he left us, the second had 'Mad Charlie' and the date he died and the third had 'Jason' and a question mark. The date was filled in on 21 June 2003.

Everyone knew Carl was on the warpath. He was hunting Moran down but I think Jason must have thought he was bulletproof.

But Carl couldn't find him. His team of nutbags that masqueraded as hitmen could have been out of a Jerry Lewis movie except they had real guns.

One of his crew was given the job of finding Jason. Now I know that bloke well, and, while he was a top stick-up man, he was hopeless at trying to follow anyone.

What made him a good stick-up man was that he had dash, had a gun and could run pretty fast. What made him no good at finding Jason was that Carl didn't even give him a picture of the target so he wouldn't have known him if they had bumped into each other at the Myer sales.

When you go to rob a bank you don't need to find it and follow it and then wait for it to be alone. You drive around until you see the word 'bank'. Then you put your balaclava on, run in, pull your gun, swear like you're on *Big Brother* and run out with the cash.

But if you are doing a hit it would be handy if you knew what the bloke you are going to kill looks like.

At one stage, Carl wanted one of his men to frock up and walk past Jason hiding his gun in a pram, then pull it out and do the business. If you knew the man who was to pull the trigger, you wouldn't want to see him in a dress. He had legs like a baboon and you would be better off waxing a sheep than trying to give him the ladies' smooth look.

They wanted to kill Jason at Mark's gravesite on the anniversary of his death but they couldn't find it on time. These boys may have been well armed but they were missing something in the brain-box region.

Finally, Carl worked out that, if you want to set someone up, watch their family. Jason's no different. He was keeping a low profile but he couldn't resist slipping out to watch his kids play junior footy.

Carl sent his team there and they waited. Jason couldn't resist wandering around like a mob boss, wearing dark glasses and shaking hands like he was Marlon Brando on a crash diet.

It was enough for the nutbag hit team to work out who he was.

The ex-armed robber was dropped off carrying three guns (as you would) and raced over to where Jason was sitting in a van and blew him away, and his little mate Pat Barbaro, too. Jason saw it coming and ducked but he had nowhere to hide. It was all over for him.

I feel really sorry for his kids who were there and saw their father and his mate die. But make no mistake, Jason was a violent gunman who copped his right whack.

When he died, some liked to say he had a heart of gold. That's crap. He had a heart of stone, although he did throw the cash around a bit to big-note when he was cashed up. That's drug money for you. It's like monopoly money.

The armed robber was supposed to get a fortune from Carl but he ended up just getting $2500. The robber ended up rolling on Williams to Purana and that was the end for Fat Carl.

The lesson is always be careful of the hired help and don't short-change gunmen.

Personally, my ambition is simply to outlive my enemies. I once said that if I got my picnic basket and sat quietly by the side of a river I would eventually see the bodies of all my enemies float by. This has happened to me. I have sat quietly by the side of the river of life and have seen the dead bodies of all my enemies drift by. This is quite an achievement: to witness the death of every living true blue enemy I have on the face of the earth, meaning every enemy who was a true blue genuine threat against me.

The deaths of Mark and Jason Moran were the deaths of the last two remaining true threats against my life. The world is full of people who verbal off about killing Chopper Read – rar rar rar. Every nitwit and their pet dog is gonna do this, that or the other to me, but men with the guts to actually carry it out and do it is another matter altogether. Mark and Jason Moran were two men who had the ability to actually do it.

It's funny but I saw Jason two weeks before he died. He was walking across Smith Street, Collingwood. He hesitated when he saw me. He had a look on his face of anger and fear. The anger of a man who wanted to kill me – and the fear of a man who wasn't carrying a loaded gun. At the time, he looked at me and nodded. I replied with a big cheerful 'How's it going, Jason?' and he replied with a paranoid half-smile and a 'How ya going, Chopper?'

I replied, 'Are you still gonna knock me, Jason?' I was standing a good ten to twelve feet from him.

'You're not worth the bother, Chopper,' he replied with his typical rapier wit.

'Don't let fear stop you, mate,' I said back with a smile and a laugh.

'I've got no blue with you, Chop,' said the man who vowed for years he'd guide me into a shallow grave.

'You should get yourself a sense of humour,' I advised him.

'I've got one,' he said back.

I told him, 'Every time I see you I laugh.'

He gave me a half-hearted smile and asked me how Peter Bosustow was going. Bosustow worked with Mark 'Jacko' Jackson and myself with *The Wild Colonial Psychos* comedy show. Bosustow was a close family friend of Moran's. I replied that Jason should ring Peter about getting work on the shows with us. Moran relaxed, sensing that if I had a gun on me I wasn't going to use it and leave him dead in the middle of Smith Street, Collingwood.

He knew the chances of my shooting him dead were very slim. He was quite right: I wasn't carrying a gun, and had I been I wouldn't have shot him in broad daylight in front of so many witnesses, anyway. Gone were those days. There was a time when I would have, but those days had long passed me by.

I chatted to him briefly about Peter Bosustow and his mood and humour began to improve and mellow. While I spoke to him, I began to walk quietly towards him. What I knew about Moran was that without a gun in his hand he couldn't fight his way out of a paper bag. The conversation ended with a handshake and he turned and walked away.

And I was left wondering what the hell the shifty bastard was doing in Collingwood in the first place. Collingwood isn't an area non-Collingwood people come to visit much as a rule. He had a handshake like a wet fish – a warm, sweaty limp handshake, very unmanly and very insincere. Had he been carrying a handgun, in spite of the daylight or the witnesses, I'm sure he would have pulled it out and shot me dead on the spot.

He was embarrassed at bumping into me, being weak enough to talk to me and being weak enough to shake my hand. He was the man who swore a death threat against me at the grave of the late Alphonse Gangitano.

My old man always said to me, 'Never trust an Aussie who takes orders off a wog.'

Sure it was a racist thing to say but the old man never wanted to be the Minister for Multiculturalism, and had made his feelings quite clear against the Japanese in World War II.

Moran was one of these dinky-di Aussies who took orders off and money from Fat Al – and lived in fear of a dagger from him. And Alphonse was a fool for trusting such a weak-gutted thing as Jason Moran. Jason was at best a woman basher and a two-bob bully boy. He never fought anyone who could fight and never made a move against anyone who had real dash or guts.

However, he was not only a coward but a sadist – which made him a dangerous mixture. He was a paranoid coward and a very egotistical sadist – which meant that with a loaded gun in his hand he would walk up to Heaven's Gate and shoot Jesus Christ himself. His actions with a gun hid the fact that the bloke couldn't fight to save himself – and was at best a gutless, woman-bashing, cowardly tip rat. But, as low as he was, Jason was the last living human being remaining who would have gunned me down in cold blood, had he been given half a chance. All in all, Carl, you did me a great favour.

Having said that, now the smoke has cleared, Carl is just another wobbly-bottomed mummy's boy who got too big for his boots. He has got a long time to think about things in jail. And when you're alone in a cell, growing old, you spend a lot of time thinking about whether it was worth playing gangsters for a few months.

But why should I care? Carl ended up with 35 years and I ended up with my worst enemies out of the way. So who is the real winner in the underworld war? You be the judge, dear reader.

PASQUALE BARBARO

*Shot in car park of the Cross Keys Hotel, Essendon North,
on 21 June 2003*

He was sitting in the van with his good friend Jason. The gunman didn't even know he was there. There are two lessons to be learned here. One, pick your friends carefully and, two, if you see some bloke running at you with a balaclava and three guns, run like stink.

WILLIE THOMPSON

*Shot dead in his car in Waverley Road, Chadstone,
on 21 July 2003*

His front was to fill vending machines at nightclubs with lollipops. His real job was selling drugs to clubbers. He was a part-time actor who was never going to make the big time after he fell out with Nik Radev.

Nik once fire-bombed his car to indicate he wasn't happy, and what did Willie go and do? He went straight out and bought a soft-top convertible as a replacement. Go figure. He should have bought an armoured van or, better yet, a ticket out of town.

He either had a hand in Nik's demise or knew that Nik was about to be set up for the hit but, if he thought his problems were over when the Bulgarian got his, he was wrong. Even though he was a very good friend of Tony Mokbel's, I suspect Carl Williams may have organised Willie's hit. It was a two-man team. The van pulled up and that was it. Classic Williams. This is probably one that Carl got away with.

MARK MALLIA

Charred body found dumped in a drain in West Sunshine on 18 August 2003

Mallia was one of that Western Suburbs crew that wanted to be a gangster. Never learned one of the most important lessons in the business. If you want to kill someone, don't announce it ahead of time.

Mallia was a mate of Nik Radev's and, after the big Bulgarian bit seven bullets with his brand-new teeth, Mark started saying he would back up for the dead drug pusher. But you can't start a war without any soldiers and Mallia was on his own. Seeing Carl organised Nik's knock, he wasn't going to wait for Mallia to get his act together so he sent his crew around. I think the last face Mark saw was Andrew Veniamin's.

It was too late to call for a time-out then.

They found the body on fire and stuffed down a drain.

Now that simply outrages the new-age Chopper. Think of what that does to the environment? Burning drug dealers must play havoc with global warning. They should have buried him and placed a nice tree on top of him. We can't let the Arctic caps melt. What would happen to all the polar bears? The ones that Bruno Grollo hasn't got stuffed and stuck in his office, anyway.

HOUSAM 'SAM' ZAYAT

Shot during a late-night meeting with a friend in a paddock in Tarneit on 9 September 2003

Another drug dealer shot dead. Who cares? Natural causes, if you ask me. And more proof that you have to watch your friends more than your enemies.

MICHAEL RONALD MARSHALL

Shot outside his home in Joy Street, South Yarra, on 25 October 2003

Now Carl Williams was really naughty with this one. Mick Marshall was just another citizen happy to sell drugs to kids so he could live the type of life he thought would suit him. His front was to sell hotdogs outside nightclubs. This put him in the perfect position to sell pills to eager young punters.

No one knew much about Marshall. He lived in a posh house in South Yarra but no one seemed to wonder how selling hotdogs and a few rolls would put him on easy street.

Tony Mokbel had a bee in his Lebanese bonnet. He was convinced Marshall had knocked his mate Willie Thompson and he went to Carl to square up. He was prepared to pay $300,000 to knock Marshall. The trouble was that Carl was the one who had Thompson bowled over so this was perfect for Fatty Williams. He'd get $300,000 and Tony would never know he was the one who had ordered Willie's shooting.

Williams gave the job to the team that had killed Jason.

While the boys had dash, they weren't blessed with too many brains. Any drug-filled idiot can pull a trigger but the stone-killer is the one who can work out the odds and knows when to walk away.

These lads thought they had a clean car to pull the job but the Purana Jacks had got there first. The driver saw the brake light was on, checked the motor and found a police tracker.

Now what would you do? Push on or pull out. You would pull out, right? You would know the police were on to you. But these two Mensa rejects decided to go on and kill Marshall anyway. Of course, the coppers were listening, and after the hit team left the hotdog man stone cold they were gobbled up by the Special Operations Group.

Tony Mokbel only had to pay the $50,000 deposit. Carl was later convicted on this one, and no wonder. Serves him right for hiring retards.

GRAHAM 'THE MUNSTER' KINNIBURGH
Shot dead outside his Kew home on 13 December 2003

The Munster should have been a winner. He was a top punter but he forgot the most important rule. Quit while you are ahead. (Or in his case while he still had one.)

He made a fortune as Australia's top safe-breaker. He could open a bank safe as easily as a tin of sardines.

He was one of the smart ones who kept a low profile. While every Victorian detective with a brain knew his name, he wasn't known to the general public. He loved the horses and a good feed and so, naturally, he was often seen eating at good restaurants with jockeys. Funny how good his inside mail was. It was one reason just about everyone liked the Munster, even some old-style coppers.

But in his younger days the Munster showed a bit of form away from the racetrack. He led a crew called the magnetic drill gang and I know he pulled a job worth nearly $2 million in NSW and a big gold haul in Queensland.

Banks around Australia had to change their safes because they were frightened the Munster would come calling with his drills.

He pulled a few big burgs and rolled over Lindsay Fox's joint. When police raided the Munster, they found Mrs Fox's unique pendant in a coat pocket. Kinniburgh beat the blister and, as I have often said, 'Thank God for juries.'

He was once charged in Sydney, and Melbourne coppers went up to give evidence. He beat the charges and when they came back the coppers were down the back drinking beer and he was on the same plane but up the front – and drinking champagne.

He used to play the mobster on his trips to Las Vegas but in Melbourne he just lived quietly in a house in Kew and put his kids through private school. People there must have thought he was a bank manager and they weren't too far wrong. He had a few, including one in Sydney, in his pocket.

I don't know whether he missed the cut and thrust of bank jobs, had a brain fade or a mid-life crisis but he started hanging out with Fat Al and that crew. That meant he was always going to end up in the headlines and all his hard work to keep in the background would be stuffed.

He was close to Lewis Moran and that meant he sometimes ran with Mark and Jason Moran. He would have been better off putting on a pair of Speedos and swimming with killer whales. It was always going to end badly. Alphonse's murder put him in prime time.

He got banned from the track and the casino so some of his biggest interests went out the window. He used to spend most of his nights down the pub looking as sour as a bloke who'd missed the fourth leg of the quaddie.

He was a good mate of Mick Gatto and his best friend was probably old Lewis Moran. Well, one thing about the Munster he could always read a form guide and he knew that, once the war was well under way, he would be on Carl's 'to do' list.

Why he didn't get in first, I'll never know. He started carrying a gun for the first time in years but he would have known it was only a matter of time. The word is he got a shot away when they came for him. He missed. They didn't.

ANDREW 'BENJI' VENIAMIN

Shot dead in the back of a Carlton restaurant
on 23 March 2004

Hitman Andrew Veniamin was shot dead by Carlton identity Mick Gatto in a Carlton restaurant. Gatto was charged with murder but was acquitted on the grounds of self-defence.

Benji was no great loss. He killed at least five blokes and he

NEVER PLEAD GUILTY

WILD COLONIAL PSYCHO'S

Psycho tour poster: Who said tent boxing is dead?

With Eddie: We Collingwood supporters stick together.

Lady kilter: It took twenty years, but Margaret and I finally got hitched.

Jacko: sharpshooter with a Sherrin, but a shotty is better.

Two smoking barrels: I have always been a stickler for firearms safety.

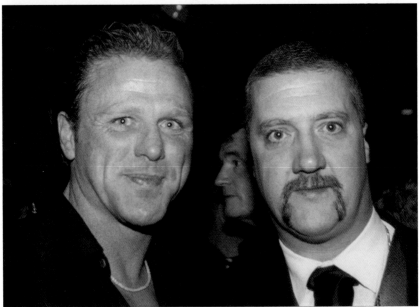

Above: Dougy Hawkins and me: champion Bulldog midfielder meets Collingwood's deadliest shot.

Below: Dermie and me: one a dangerous psychopath, the other did 23 years' jail.

Above: From B Division to the A list: Margaret, me and kickboxing legend Stan 'The Man' Longinidis.

Below: With Bernie Jackson … Jacko's better half, by a long way.

A stylish couple: red is a good fashion choice for me; it matches my blood.

Above: Framed: I've done some painting but I won't plead guilty to this.

Below: Multi-skilling: Archibald Prize-winning artist Adam Cullen brushed up my painting but I promise I didn't teach him about guns.

Above: Cheers: Former ace detective 'Rocket Rod' Porter recommends Melbourne Bitter when old friends meet.

Below: Fears: Former ace gunman Amos Atkinson prefers the traditional VB after a hard day's skulduggery.

Running red hot: Chili Peppers top banana Anthony Kiedis wondering if I'll give him an autograph.

Above: The best retired burglar, television host, street fighter, and former standover man in Collingwood: Sean Lang, Kenny Pennant and me with a bloke in a suit.

Below: Hands on: I call my Albanian bodyguards Anger and Sorrow. Guess why?

Above: Meet and greet: Jacko and me with a bloke who said he's the singer from Jamiroquai. Sounds like a cocktail.

Below: Twins: only our mothers can tell us apart, except Aka is a little under his fighting weight and I am in peak condition.

Above: Back to back: award-winning artist and top-selling author. And they said we'd never make it.

Below: The ultimate rope-a-dope … Andrew Denton: popular entertainer who could be the new Bert Newton. A true personal friend.

Above: Barnesy, Margy and Choppy. All we need is a drummer.

Below: Barnesy and friends: drag queens in Pentridge were never like this.

Read and Rogerson Inc: we no longer catch and kill our own, but we remember how.

must have been on drugs if he thought he could go up against Mick Gatto.

Gatto was a real lion and Benji was a mangy Maltese cross with dreams of being a tiger.

I have known Mick for 30 years and he was everything Alphonse Gangitano wanted to be. Legitimately brave, tough and calm, he didn't need to bash people to get respect or prove he was a tough guy. People just knew he was a man who when he talked you listened. Now Mick was always the enterprising type and he ran the two-up for years. He didn't do much jail time and that was because he was smart enough to keep ahead of the posse.

As they get older, crooks with a brain look to move out of the world of cops and robbers and branch into business. I myself moved into the world of the arts, writing, movies and painting – subjects that fit my sensitive nature.

Mick moved into mediation and problem solving. I thought that was a perfect fit with his skills and temperament.

Then he got dragged into the Carl Williams fiasco. Mick was going sort of legit. He had nothing to do with the drug business. He left that to the bottom dwellers, but Williams was so shit frightened of Mick he thought the Big Fella would come after him. That's why he was desperate to see Mick dead.

They had a meeting at the casino to try to sort things out. Why the casino? It is a nice open place with plenty of cameras. No one pulls an ambush when there are closed-circuit videos everywhere so it can be a good place to chat.

Mick told Carl that as far as he was concerned he would

keep out of what was going on, but if Carl was stupid enough to come looking he would end up second best.

Williams should have listened but dickheads like Benji said they should go after Mick.

It was like a rubber duckie raising the attack flag to a battleship. It was only going to end one way.

Carl wanted Veniamin to do the job and he certainly had the track record. He had fixed up Frank Benvenuto, Dino Dibra, Nik Radev and Paul Kallipolitis and Victor Peirce for sure and probably had a hand in a few others, too.

But, with respect to that crew, they were lightweights and middleweights, while Mick was a true heavyweight. I have always admired Mick. Unlike many of the Carlton Crew, he has real dash and doesn't need to show off with unnecessary violence. But, when he gets cross, someone gets sad.

The really tough man doesn't need to prove it. The gangster who pistol whips a nobody when he has his team around him to back him up does it because he is trying to prove to himself that he is not a coward. And, no matter how many times he does it, the truth never changes. When faced with a true enemy, he soils his nappies. The number of times Chopper has had to listen to so-called tough men crying when they are on the receiving end makes me want to throw up in an airsick bag.

Some of the biggest gangsters turn to pussycats when in jail and they don't have their crew with them to make them look good.

Once I heard the word that Benji might be gunning for Mick, I knew it was only going to end one way. And deep down so did Veniamin. He told police that he expected that he was going to get knocked.

It was only a matter of picking the time and the place. Andrew lost the plot – so they put him in one.

He forgot the old rule: a good big man always beats a good little one.

Tiny little Benji was silly to try and pick on a giant like Mick Gatto. Of course, it was a clear-cut case of self-defence.

Gatto was at his usual table at his favourite restaurant in Carlton when Veniamin walked in and sat down. Now to get between Mick and his veal scaloppini is a dangerous move at the best of times, but during an underworld war it was a downright stupid.

Many people have dined with Mick when they have had a problem and often (for a substantial fee) they get a good feed of pasta and their problems fixed at the same time.

But this was different. There would be no time for chit-chat and dessert-of-the-day.

According to Mick, Veniamin kicked him under the table and said he wanted to see him privately. Kick Mick? Why would he do that? But Gatto said it happened so it must have.

The two men walked to a small area next to the kitchen, well away from prying eyes.

Apparently, Veniamin went in first to the dead-end corridor, which meant he had no plans of an ambush at that point.

It was such a narrow area that, if Mick had fallen the wrong way, it would have blocked his escape. Plus there were several of Mick's best mates at the table who would have been able to back up there and then.

Veniamin left his car keys and mobile phone on the table so he obviously hadn't planned a shooting. You can hardly kill the boss and then go back to the table and ask for your keys so you can make a quick getaway.

So what happened in there?

There was an argument. That's for sure. Mick said later that Veniamin pulled a gun and fired a shot. He then took the gun off Benji and shot him dead.

Now Benji was in no position to argue as he had lost interest in the matter once he was shot twice in the neck and once in the head. A good .38 will do that.

Mick came out after the shooting, apologised about the bother and declared that Veniamin had said he'd killed 'Graham' and then 'he tried to kill me'.

Benji could hardly quibble.

Now it may have looked bad for Mick but I had no doubt he would be acquitted. Because, you must remember, dear reader, the survivor always owns the crime scene.

I have been involved in several complex self-defence cases and have always come out in front.

In June 1987, I shot drug dealer Sammy the Turk (Siam Ozerkam) dead outside Bojangles Nightclub in St Kilda by popping him in the left eye from point-blank range with a little sawn-off .410 shotgun and the jury agreed with me that it was self-defence. I think they would have been given a medal if they could.

I agree with Mick that it must have been self-defence. It would probably be churlish to raise the fact he had a body bag in the boot of his car, but I suppose, like a good boy scout, he was just being prepared.

While Mick may have had no choice that day, it did put out a message – that he wasn't going to pay underworld mice to do his dirty work and, if the other side wanted to come after him, then they had better be prepared to suffer the consequences.

Compare that to Tony Mokbel – a fat idiot with too much money and too much time on his hands. Mokbel always got others to do the killing for him and hid in the shadows – Mick cast his own shadow and didn't need to hide behind others.

Now Gatto was arrested at the scene and was locked up in solitary confinement for 14 months. I reckon you can tell a lot about someone on how they do jail time. Most of the plastic gangsters go to water once inside, but Mick just got on with it. He lost thirty kilos inside by shadow boxing. I was never as fit as when I was inside, bench pressing massive weights and eating healthy foods. The trouble is on the outside there are so many distractions that the fitness campaigns are always the first casualty.

Gatto went to the Supreme Court, gave evidence, looked straight at the jury and told them he should be given the keys to the city for getting rid of someone like Veniamin. Of course, he was right and the jury agreed.

He was acquitted and left, his reputation undamaged by

scallywag suggestions and foul rumour that he had the gun hidden in the corridor and Veniamin was unarmed. Perish the thought – and perish the hitman.

I do know that, when Margaret and I wanted to see the Rolling Stones, I had a chat to Mick's very good friend Dave 'The Rock' Hedgcock. Dave was Alphonse's old bodyguard but we are all allowed a few mistakes in our life. I had breakfast recently with him and another old Melbourne legend: karate expert Bob Jones. Dave is heavily involved in the security industry and was able to organise a couple of tickets for me and Margaret to go to the Rolling Stones. They were in the VIP section about six from the front. I was told Mick Gatto had a helping hand in that. I gave both of them one of my boxing paintings that I'm told hang in their homes.

Mick still knows a lot of people.

LEWIS MORAN

Shot dead in the Brunswick Club, Sydney Road,
31 March 2004

Lewis Moran was a mean old pickpocket who began pumping the drugs out when his stepson Mark and son Jason showed him what sort of money you could make.

Lewis was savage on a dollar. Cash was his God and he would pull the coat of the Devil if he thought there was a quid in it.

He was a top thief and could work the races as good as anyone, but, when he started to be spoken of as a Mr Big,

I knew that the mice were now the kings of the jungle.
Like his kids, Moran loved to pull a shooter, as long as he
knew the other guy was A) pissed, B) unarmed, C) a pacifist,
D) a squarehead.

He never went up against anyone who would fight back.
He was another one of his crew who would blab on about
getting the Chopper but I think he did his best work under
the doona.

When his kids got bowled over, he finally decided it was
time to get Carl and he offered a contract but he was so tight
he was only prepared to stump up $40,000, even though
Williams and Mokbel were saying they would pay up to
$200,000 (even though they lashed some of their teams and
didn't cough up the cash). (The sap who shot Jason got $2500
in the hand. I get more for a painting. And there's less mess to
clean up too.)

Some would think that, with all that money, Lewis would
have had a great life. But he was always just a sour old turd.
He would spend most of his days watching the cooking
channel on cable TV and looking for new recipes. I think in
the end he didn't even like horses too much even though he
was an old SP.

Everyone knew Lewis was not long for the world. He tried
to carry a shooter but Light Fingered Lewis had arthritis and
could no longer carry a gun.

Even one of the main Purana detectives, Filthy Phil
Swindells, jumped the witness box to get Moran's bail curfew
changed so he wasn't going home at the same time, which

would make him a sitting duck for a hit. Filthy Phil is generous like that, but he couldn't save Lewis from himself.

Moran seemed to have lost the will to survive and he went to the Brunswick Club for a beer every night even though Mr Magoo with a water pistol could have popped him off.

He used to get his beer cheap and that was enough for tight old Lewis. As long as his beer had a good head, he didn't seem to worry that he was able to get his shot off.

Now, I happen to know one of the men who pleaded guilty to the murder. He told the police his team was promised $150,000 from Mokbel and Williams for the hit and was shortchanged $10,000. It must have been GST (Gun Shot Tax).

Lewis had been married to Judy Moran. Judy's first husband, Leslie Cole, was shot dead outside his Sydney home in November 1982.

Cole was Mark's real father, which was why he looked nothing like Jason.

So Judy lost two husbands and two sons in four murders. That has to be some sort of record, even in Melbourne.

She wrote a book after all the funerals. If you missed it, you can pick it up in the science-fiction section of those places where you buy books for 50 cents a kilo.

Judy even tried to bag The Chopper but as I always say, 'Sticks and stones can break your bones but bullets kill your family.'

She bags me, but I didn't kill her kids.

I saw a picture of her crying after Jason was plugged and you had to feel for her but then she puts the war paint on and turns up at all the Moran funerals like some sort of creature from another galaxy.

Hey, Judy. Why don't you put your hand up?

You can marry one no-hoper, but two?

And how come both your sons turned out to be violent, vindictive, drug-dealing, scum-sucking, weak-gutted fools?

Did you ever try and stop them? No.

Judy, when you were heading off on a five-star holiday or going to the Flower Drum to get a gutful of beef chow-mein and oysters and French bubbly, did you ever wonder where the money came from? Judy was the most dangerous of all the Morans, particularly when armed with chopsticks if you got between her and a hot wok of Mongolian lamb.

When Jason came home from jail and started driving a silver BMW, did you think he got that from the Parole Board for being prisoner of the year?

When you turned up at Jason's funeral, you said, 'All will be dealt with, my darling.'

How dumb was that? It was a clear message to Carl and his crew to keep going or your mob would come after them. Best if you had stuck to sticking a dim sim in your mouth when you opened it instead of making statements that get your family and his friends knocked.

And then, after Williams finally pleaded guilty to four murders, you complained because they dropped the one for killing Mark.

You bleated that Williams had killed most of your family but you seemed to have forgotten that it was your boys who started it when they shot Carl in the guts back in 1999.

They started it, but they didn't have the dash to back up.

You called for the hangman to be brought out of retirement. Funny, I didn't hear you calling for capital punishment when Jason was in the frame for Alphonse's murder.

Judy wrote in her 'book' that she wanted to thank her barber for the hairstyles she wore to all the funerals and the person who gave her lovely shoes. What a fashion statement – crocodile tears while wearing crocodile shoes. God help us all.

No one took Judy too seriously. That's why Lewis pissed off on her years ago. At least he got that right.

LEWIS CAINE

Shot dead and body dumped in Brunswick on 8 May 2004

For a start – who the bloody hell was 'Lewis fucking Caine?'

When he starts getting mentioned as some sort of underworld heavyweight, then the mice have taken over the jungle.

I was in H Division with Lewis Caine – he was just a fucking weak-gutted idiot when I first met him and hadn't grown in status or reputation since then.

He was also an alleged karate expert who kicked some harmless bloke to death for looking twice at his girlfriend.

Caine entered Pentridge under a cloud of suspension along with a storm of laughter.

My old enemy in prison, a man I will call CIA, was on a recruitment drive and Caine put his hand up and quickly joined his crew and then shit himself when he got put into the same shower yard as my good self. In H Division Pentridge, all he got from me was my foot up his arse as he scurried out of the shower yard almost in tears.

It is hard for me to believe that anyone would have offered Lewis Caine a contract to kill anyone. What I can believe is that CIA would eventually shoot his one-time friend for money.

I also knew CIA's criminal ego couldn't allow him to sit on the sidelines while the biggest underworld gang war in Melbourne criminal history is going on without him being involved in some way, shape or form.

I was told that he was ringing around trying to get a foot in the door of either camp. The Italians no longer trusted him – and he was trying to get his head in with the Carl Williams Western Suburbs mob.

So stupid Caine hopped in a car with CIA and his crew. Did he think they were going to the drive-in to see a double feature?

Talk about Dancing with Wolves. Or in this case Driving with Ferrets.

TERENCE HODSON AND CHRISTINE HODSON

Shot dead in their Kew home on 15 May 2004

Talkative Terry was a police informer and it was the worst-kept secret in Melbourne. No one with a brain trusted Terry and then he ended getting arrested with a drug squad detective doing a burg on an amphetamines lab. That was pretty good proof that he was working with the coppers. Then he rolled again and started working with the anti-corruption police against his former partners.

I don't think that would have made him too popular.

A few police documents were leaked to the crooks to prove he was an informer. It was like berley to fish, encouraging them into a feeding frenzy.

Terry always had good security but that night he let his killer in so you can guess it was a friend who did the shooting. Another case of never trusting those close to you. His wife was killed because she knew too much.

Who was behind this appalling crime? Probably a regular at the old police picnics, I would think. Certainly fuel for thought.

LEE PATRICK TORNEY

Found down a mineshaft on 6 March 2006

Lee Torney was another street fighter who lost his dash when he was locked up in H Division. It's funny how many big men become little men when they have to do hard jail time. Lee killed a mate named Sidney Graham back in 1982. Silly Sid punched a hole in his manners at a party when he started complaining about his cut in a bank robbery.

Lee later told him they had another job – he just forgot to mention the job was to kill Sid. Fair enough, too. Sid might not have been that enthusiastic if he knew the truth.

Anyway, Torney took Grizzling Graham out into the bush and shot him. It worked. Sid never complained again.

When Torney got out after 11 years, he still wanted to be the two-bob gangster, playing around with guns and growing a bit of dope up the country.

He went missing in 2005 and I thought back then it would end in tears because people like Lee don't just run off to join the circus. They found his body, or what was left of it, about a year later down a mineshaft. Call me a cynic but I doubt if he was out mushrooming and just fell down the hole. I suspect someone helped him find the bottom.

The funny thing is that after Lee's funeral they found that they had forgotten his head, which was still down at the coroner's office.

It wasn't a big problem because Lee was never a deep thinker.

MARIO CONDELLO

Shot dead as he returned to his Brighton home
on 6 February 2006

Williams was in jail, Veniamin was dead and all the Morans that mattered were no longer with us, so you would have thought all the fun and games were over. But there was one more surprise – the murder of Mario Condello.

Condello was a big man and Mick Gatto's offsider. In fact, when Mick was in jail for a 14-month rest (and fitness programme) waiting for his trial over Veniamin, it was Condello who had to run things. Mick wrote to him from jail and gave him instructions but Condello had to walk the walk.

Sure he looked the part. He dressed in Lygon Street black and could have had a walk-on role with *The Sopranos* if he wanted but I never saw him as having Mick's guts.

Condello was smart – no question about that. He had been a qualified lawyer until he was struck off over a few trifling matters like drug dealing and arson. He served six years for that, which can put a hole in your work CV.

Mario wanted to be a gangster but he also wanted to be a judge at one time. Bit hard to do both unless your name is Lionel Murphy, I reckon.

Condello was on bail and about to have his trial on planning to kill Carl Williams. I have no doubt he would have beaten the charges but we'll never know now.

His trial was about to start and the courts had ordered he be home every night by 10pm.

For any killer worth his salt, that was just perfect. You don't have to do all the homework on your victim. You know what time he has to be home so you can just sit off and wait.

Tick-tock then bang-bang. Then it's off home in time for a hot chocolate and the late news.

Mario spent nine months in solitary before he was bailed over the Williams plot and he came out half a broken man. Mick did his time easy but I suspect it was too much for Mario.

Some people can do mainstream jail easy but solitary plays with their head. After more than twenty years in the hardest jails in Australia, believe me – I know.

Mario was a blood and guts man. His guts and someone else's blood – as long as it didn't touch his manicured fingers. He was another in a long line who was happy to order others to take the risks but wasn't too keen on seeing the end product.

The closest he got to the blood was the chance of a nasty paper cut when signing dud cheques.

So who killed him? I would suggest Carl was on the way out by then and didn't have the pull. Half his crew was turning on him and he had his own problems.

But Tony Mokbel was still about and Tony still blamed Mario for the beating he got in Lygon Street. It was supposed to be a peace conference and Tony got jumped and bashed. Tony blamed Mario for that.

Both Mario and Tony were money men and Tony was the richest one. Money talks all languages – but particularly Italian and Lebanese.

Another thing, Carl had a direct line to Victoria's most dangerous stone-killer – a man mentioned over many murders but never charged.

The killing of Mario was text-book. The victim drove into his garage and before the electric doors closed the gunmen was in, did the job and was out.

That was no apprentice – it was the professional.

At the funeral, there were 600 at the church. It was further proof that the Carlton Crew was going to stick fat. It was a message that Mick Gatto's crew were not going anywhere.

For Carl and Tony, it was a parting shot.

Muhammad Ali was one of the greatest boxers the world has seen, but in the end he stood there getting the shit punched out of him by people who weren't fit to empty his spit bucket. Ted Whitten had to have his coat pulled and told it was time to give the game away. Dennis Lillee stopped bowling, lost his hair and started doing carpet ads.

So what has this to do with the underworld war? What I am getting at is you can beat murder charges, you can beat the coppers and you can beat your enemies but you can never beat the clock.

When the bodies started dropping, there were some blokes of my generation who wanted a piece of it.

There is nothing more pathetic than some over-the-hill, middle-aged has been still trying to pretend that he is a tough guy. And one of those who turned killer is a prime example of this.

I have mentioned this turkey to you already. I have known him for thirty years: he wasn't much good in his prime and age hasn't improved him. He was born an imbecile and has been losing ground ever since.

We went to war years ago in Pentridge and, while he had the numbers, I had the psychopaths, so you know who won.

The courts have told me I can't name him, so I will keep calling him CIA, because that's the initials I gave him a few pages back. Remember?

Anyway, CIA was born to be a criminal and all his family were thieves and murders. He thought of himself as an underworld aristocrat but I bet his dead relatives would be rolling in their graves at what CIA has become.

The problem with CIA is he loves the headlines but hates the jail time involved and will pull every stunt he can think of or tell any lie he has to tell or point the finger at whoever else he could in order to avoid a sentence. His usual method is to talk one of his co-accused into putting his hand up for the murder or the shooting. That's correct; more than once CIA has talked one of his co-accused into taking the full blame when he is the one who has pulled the trigger.

He is quite brilliant in his ability to talk other people into helping him out and has been talking men and women into believing in him and his lost causes for years.

He is a criminal conman who launches into massive verbal games with men younger than himself. All those his own age and older are awake to him. He always plays to a much younger criminal and pulls them into his psychological web. Generally, it is one of these starry-eyed poor stooges who agrees to put their hands up in the air.

For years, he said he was an enemy of mine but when he got out he made a trip to Tassie where I was living at the time to see if we were squared away.

I wished him no harm and hoped he would retire like me, but when the shooting started and the money was flying around CIA couldn't resist sticking his giant hooter into the middle of it all. I'm sure the old fool thought he could slip through the middle, playing both sides off against each other, and when they were all gone he would be the winner.

That was always him – an ego that didn't match his ability.

He offered himself up as a hitman, which didn't surprise me but what shocked me was that some idiots were prepared to entertain his offers.

He and his team of dickheads killed Lewis Moran and Lewis Caine (must have hated the name Lewis) but they were in the frame for both and it was only a matter of time until the police came knocking. And true to form CIA started trying to do the best deal he could for himself and stuff the rest of them.

The Carlton Crew wouldn't have hired him, as they know his true form only too well. It only tells me whoever involved him had to be a younger crew with no memory of his real criminal history.

I'm reliably informed it was CIA who hawked his services around in the first place. So CIA knocked on drug dealer's door crying poor, begging for work.

Anyway, CIA was promised $150,000 to knock Lewis Moran and, after the job, his team got $140,000.

But in crime terms CIA was an old man and, faced with spending the rest of his life in jail, he turned informer, pleaded guilty and gave his two bosses up in the hope he got a sentence that would get him out before he was dead.

If Williams had asked me, I would have told him how it would end up. He always got caught and then he always looked after himself.

CIA turned dog so quickly it was amazing. But I've always known this about him. He was the one who turned Alphonse Gangitano against me. Alphonse thought CIA was a member of the Victorian Federated Ship Painters and Dockers, but now we find out he never even held a Dockies brief.

He controlled 300 Painters and Dockers in Pentridge Prison through his friendship with Johnny 'Piggy' Palmer who was a Painter and Docker and back then a very powerful and respected member of the docks fraternity, having beaten the Car-O-Tel Motel double murder back in the 1970s.

Barry Robert Quinn wore that, but he kept his mouth shut, unlike the crims of today.

I went to war with Piggy and CIA in H Division and they called me a dog. That's all it took back then. No one has ever spent a night in prison over a Chopper deal; not a day, a night or a single hour has any one spent in prison over me. In those days, some saw him as an underworld hero – some staunch, old-school crook taught the right way by generations of Dockies. He shouldn't have been at Pentridge, but down the road at the showgrounds. He would have won the gold medal for the best dog award.

CIA has been doing secret deals with the police for over thirty years and now it is all out in the open. Too late for me, but not for him. I still believe revenge will be mine. Every day I wake up in my own bed is a win. CIA will have to be protected and will look over his shoulder for the rest of his miserable life.

Let's make it clear it took about twenty-four years for the penny to drop with me. I kept doing crime and jail time but eventually even I realised it was over for me.

Sure there were a few who would have liked me to get involved this time around but that was never going to happen.

A few years earlier, my crew, including Mad Charlie and Dave the Jew, would have sat off, said nothing and then killed a few from either side just to keep it interesting. We would have put another log on the fire. But not now. Charlie's dead and Dave and I have retired. At least, I have.

When I was the best of my time it was because I didn't care if I lived or died. That made me the most dangerous lunatic in the asylum.

The bomber you most fear is the one with the bomb strapped to him. If he is prepared to die to kill you, then you are in serious bother.

Back then I was unmarried and without kids. What I did was for my team and me. I was the general with a group of insane soldiers who would go anywhere and do anything.

But once you have kids you don't want to lose and then you can't win.

Half these blokes got popped going home. They wanted to live the lives of family men and be killers as well. You can't do both. Once I had kids I was out of it.

I watched from the front row but I would no longer get in the ring. That is for young men with no brains and no futures.

I would rather have a cup of tea and a good lie-down these days. I knew when this started all I had to do was watch and wait.

I would be a winner without lifting a trigger finger.

We all think it was better in our day but when fat wogs are

getting people killed it's time to pack up and become a Scientologist like Tom Cruise.

A fat Lebanese Wombat with a taste in gold jewellery and a truckload of amphetamine chemicals, Tony started believing his own publicity and started acting like Doctor Evil.

Funny, after the Perth bikies bashed him in Lygon Street, he didn't try to back up against them. The bikies from the Wild West tend to blow you up and your family with you, so he stayed around Melbourne where he thought he was the master of the universe.

He was making a fortune but he wanted to be the puppet master and use Williams to do his dirty work.

They were doing all right at one stage because their men were getting knocked and a dead man can't tell tales. But, when they started recruiting older crooks it was always going to end badly. They could do the crime but not the time and were certainties to roll over and become police witnesses.

Mokbel did a runner in 2006 but I always predicted they would get him in the end and he'll spend most of his life in jail. No Ferraris, no French champagne. Just three bad meals a day and rancid tea in a chipped mug.

If I had been about, I would have shown him how good the paint job is on a Ferrari by putting him in the boot of one to reflect on his ways.

Funny thing is, his girlfriend's family are very close to one of Victoria's best stone-killers and yet he has never been mentioned in any of the murders. I bet The Duke has his fingerprints all over more than one of the jobs.

Williams ran around taunting the coppers and posing for pictures in the papers. He should have spent more time learning history than being a show pony. Military killers wear camouflage not iridescent lime green. Ever heard of the stealth bomber? It's not painted fucking hot pink, numb-nut.

If Carl had kept his head down and wiped out all his enemies, then he had a chance. But the longer it went, the less chance he had.

The police and the government couldn't let this go on. When I was asked on TV how the police would go, I said they would get a new coffee machine, a new computer and some new cars and solve stuff all. Well, that might have been a good funny for the six o'clock news but I was wrong, and I'm happy to admit it. How was I to know that Carl would hire such give-ups as CIA? If you hire rats, they'll give you the plague in the end.

Good luck to the coppers, they broke the code of silence that had lasted since it came off the convict ships more than 200 years ago.

The good old Aussie criminal code is dead and I'm glad I'm out of it.

I've noticed with a sense of personal shame that no Italians have turned dog during the years this war has been going on. No secret deals with the police, no evidence given in court by any Italians, no deals done by any Italians and no Italians applying for the witness protection programme.

The Italians have been staunch, solid, stand-up guys, honest and true to their word. They have in a criminal sense conducted themselves during all the years of death and mayhem with honour. I write this with a real sense of personal shame as a true blue Aussie criminal or former criminal: that the only dogs in this fight have all come from the Aussie side.

Yes, Carl won the bloody war: at $250,000 a hit, cash up front, how could he not? But he only bought the deaths of his enemies; he didn't buy the silence of the person who pulled the trigger.

The Italians, on the other hand, as a rule don't hire hitmen. They get their nephews or their cousins or brothers or uncles or personal friends of the family to do the hit. The loyalty of the killer has to be without question before they even ask, let alone hand over any money. Loyalty and friendship has to be first examined very carefully before any business can be spoken of. Carl Williams, on the other hand, was hiring any two-bob, over-the-hill, has-been junkie, police informer willing to say yes for $250,000 cash up front.

You idiot, Carl. You hired fucking wombats, losers, dogs and lying weak mice that took your money then sold you down the drain. It was your own fault and you'll have more than thirty years to think about it.

Mokbel used his own family and they stuck fat. But he bought the loyalty of others. Slowly they are taking away that loyalty by seizing all his property and cash. Then they put a $1 million bounty on his head.

Money to crooks is like cheese to mice – they can't resist it.

I was tempted to say, 'Give me a passport, a map of Europe and a couple of handguns and I'd have a go at finding him myself.' Was that reward for dead or alive?

Was I ever asked to get involved? Well, seriously, let me say, if I had been, the answer would have been no.

I have been short of cash and declared bankrupt in 2006. (How embarrassing, being raided by an elite team of bookkeepers wearing cardigans and Hush Puppies and armed with calculators.) But no matter how broke I am, I will not hop back into the underworld.

If I had been asked back a few years ago, it would have been over in a week. Bang, bang, bang. Don't drag this shit out as it gives people too much time to think. Do it quick and clean and then we can go to the footy at the weekend.

But I can tell you police questioned me after many of the murders. I still don't know whether they seriously thought I was a suspect, whether they were going through the motions or they were simply curious to have a chat with a true professional. Former professional, that is.

After all, as I said, I had done a spooky bit of forecasting by putting Jason's grave on the back cover of one of my books years before he stepped in the hole.

When the police knocked on the door, it was almost comical. My wife had Tim Tam biscuits for them every time they came calling. I had to tell her to ease up on the Tim Tams. It was costing us a fortune and was playing havoc with my waistline.

My son from my first marriage, Charlie, came to Melbourne to visit me for my 50th birthday and met his little brother. He loves his little brother and whenever I ring Charlie up he always asks me how baby brother is going. I'm glad the two brothers know each other because in time to come they will only have each other. Charlie is at the age where he asks me tough questions such as, Do I love baby brother more than him?

He has also started to ask me things like: 'Dad, how many people have you shot and killed?' Now I have looked in all the advice columns in magazines and I have not found an answer for how to handle that curly question.

Now, I have been known to brag every now and again but for the sake of my family I will have to start playing down my record. You can't say to your kids, 'I've shot nineteen people and iron-barred about another thirty so eat your broccoli if you want to grow up big and strong.'

I still haven't given up hope of pulling the Father of the Year Award – after all, Bob Hawke won it once, so I've got to have a chance.

As Charlie and his little bro get older, the amount of people I've shot will become smaller and smaller. I can see the day where the amount I've shot will be the exact amount I've been arrested for: Johnny Carroll, Chris Liapas, Sidney Michael Collins – of which I was convicted but pleaded not guilty. And Sammy the Turk, who I was found not guilty of murdering. Four shooting charges in one life isn't a real lot at all, if you say it quickly. Hardly worth a second mention. I never thought I'd have to answer such questions put to me by my own young son and I must admit I found myself in a dilemma.

The last time I was a serious suspect for a murder was when the former President of the Outlaws Motor Cycle Club, Silly Sid Collins, went missing. Students of the *Chopper* series will remember that I was charged with shooting Collins in 1992 in Tasmania. I still can't admit to that shooting as I'd get fifteen years for perjury.

It took a long time but I knew Karma, armed with an untraceable handgun, would eventually catch up with Sid. He went missing in NSW in 2001 and has not been seen since – and I wouldn't be holding my breath that one day he will wander out of the bush claiming a bad case of amnesia.

On the topic of Sidney Michael Collins, the former president of the Outlaws, I am reliably informed that I'm the only human being to have ever shot a motorcycle club president and lived to tell the story. The fact that I still to this day maintain my innocence over this shooting – and the fact that Collins turned crown witness against me to get me put away under the Dangerous Criminal's Act in Tasmania – is probably part of the reason I'm still alive.

Motorcycle club presidents are not meant to give people up in police stations and in courts of law over a shooting incident.

Collins broke the code of silence – and broke his own club code of honour – when he gave evidence against me in the Tasmanian Supreme Court.

Hence, I am still alive to tell the story of how I did not shoot Sidney Michael Collins. Ha ha. Whether I did or I didn't it's all academic now. I was convicted over his shooting and I cannot write that I shot the dirty little tip-rat as that would mean a charge of telling fibs in court and we wouldn't want that.

The fact that everyone takes it for granted that I really did shoot Collins is neither here nor there. I cannot help what people believe and if people wish to believe foul gossip and slander I cannot help it. All I can do is to repeat for good legal reasons that I pleaded not guilty to his shooting and I will always maintain my innocence in relation to this matter.

I also had nothing to do with his death and disappearance in Casino, NSW. He was, after all, allegedly involved with the Russian Mafia – which is, in fact, the Albanian Mafia – in the importation of Russian brides.

That group would get Russian girls to marry men with Australian citizenship and bring them to Australia. The Russian ladies, all of whom happened to be physically beautiful, would be put to work in Australian brothels, which is one way to spend your honeymoon in an exotic foreign country, I guess. Collins somehow got himself involved, and – according to rumour – fell foul of the people he was dealing with.

When these people get cross, you don't get one over your grave as you are buried in an unmarked one – in this case near a farm in country Victoria, it is said.

I can assure you all – it was nothing to do with me, although I might know some people who know some people who knew some people who sold some people a couple of Albanian shovels.

Remember 'at the end of the day' it's night time. Ha ha.

As for Sidney Michael Collins — what can I say — when the one great scorer comes to mark against your name it's not if you won or lost but how you played the game. That's one way of looking at it. Personally my ambition is simply to outlive my enemies.

I was also questioned over Nik Radev and Victor Peirce and even asked about my knowledge of the murder of hitman and all-round imbecile Christopher Dale Flannery in Sydney.

I should be on a retainer — or at least get my Tim Tams for nothing.

I asked the police how many times since 1971 they have questioned me for the murder and they came back and said, 'Forty-five times, Chopper.'

I should get valet parking at the St Kilda Road police station and my own squad stubbie holder.

I told them that, even if my memory is fading in middle age, I'm pretty sure I haven't killed all those people. 'We know that,' was the reply. Then why are you here committing grievous bodily harm on my Tim Tams? 'Because in each and every case you have known the victims,' they said.

I thought about it and they were right. I have known forty-five people who are no longer with us today.

In some of the cases, I couldn't care less, in others, I am absolutely delighted, and in some cases I am sad, as good friends have gone.

I see that list of dead and realise how half of my life was wasted playing a game with real bullets and real blood. I see the list and am relieved I am not on it. Through a combination of bullets, balls, bravery, brains, bullshit and plain dumb luck I walked though a hail of gunfire and out the other side.

I've been questioned for thirty-three shootings in Melbourne where they have all lived and got to hospital without giving me up. I've been questioned for thirty-three: I only did about eleven of them myself. As for murders, if you want the truth, the whole truth and nothing but the truth, all bullshit lies and leg-pulling aside, I've killed no more than four people personally and been present when another three were put off. All the rest are about what racing stewards call 'prior knowledge'. Like Robbie Waterhouse and Fine Cotton.

Anyway, back to Williams. He won the war, but lost the chess game. He had the body count on his side, but the brain count was on Mick Gatto's side.

During my war with Alphonse back in 1987, when Fat Al fled to Italy to escape me, Mick never had a harsh word for me. He knew it was not his war and that is where Carl made his great mistake. He thought Mick would come after him because of his blue with the Morans. He was wrong. Mick would have seen that Mark and Jason started it so he would have let the bodies fall where they did. He was wise and Carl was a fool. And when Carl went after Gatto it was a fat and sulky labrador up against a battle-hardened pit bull.

The funny thing is there are two winners out of the war. One wasn't involved and the other was a reluctant player.

Gatto had long worked out that his future was in mediation and cranes, not murder and standover crap. He did his best work in a suit over lunch, not down back lanes. But he was dragged into it and did what he had to do to make sure he never again had to look over his shoulder.

Williams has lost. He killed more but now he will spend most of the rest of his life in jail. As the caravan moves on, he will be remembered in old newspaper files and books like this. He will get old and younger prisoners who want to make a name for themselves will bash him. If he survives, he will end up in protection or working in the prison library. If he gets out, he will be an old frightened man who will have a panic attack just crossing the road. All his friends and hangers-on will have gone.

I will say one thing for Carl. He cut a deal and pleaded guilty. But he didn't turn dog. He could have got a big discount if he had become a police witness but no one is doing jail time because of him. Even when the Morans shot him in 1999, he kept his mouth shut and decided to do his own dirty work.

Unlike Mokbel, you have to say, he has had the dash to pull the trigger at least once. The only time Tony lifted his hand was to sign a cheque.

So Mick was the winner. He came out of jail thirty kilos and a few friends lighter but he is still in business.

And there is another winner. One who sat back and did nothing.

As I have said before, I intended to picnic on the side of the river and watch the bodies of my enemies float by. 'Look, there goes another one… pass me a delicious chicken wing.'

Alphonse said he'd get me and he's dead and then the Morans said they'd get me and they are all gone.

So, thanks, Carl. You did me a big favour.

I'd visit you in jail but I don't care for prisons much these days. They are far too depressing.

CHAPTER 3

GANGLANDS

There is no such thing in the underworld as 'mates'

There is a never-ending supply of evil. Don't worry, boys and girls, there is enough out there for all of us.

What if the author was to tell a story about a small crew of professional killers whose weapons, ammo and tactics were all provided by the all-time greatest professional hitman in Australian criminal history? It would be a very hard story to believe.

However, bear in mind two things. One is that the hitman is the author's best, oldest and dearest friend and is also a great reader and lover of books.

The other is that a smart reader might notice that there has been a series of underworld murders in Australia that have coincided with the release of certain books.

It follows the same pattern. A month or so before the release of the author's next book, or a month or so after, there would be a high-profile underworld murder. There would be front-page headlines about underworld wars and the press would turn to the author for his comments. Each time there would be a mention of his latest books and the result would be seen in book sales.

He would make a killing... so to speak.

The police receive all their information from criminals and, believe it or not, the media, which also gather information from criminals and police. It's like a ladies' sewing circle, all swapping gossip.

I'm talking about matters strictly underworld. When a criminal identity is killed, it is not a matter the general public can help with, such as a missing person, a bank robbery, a rape, an abducted child or the murder of some poor little old lady.

A criminal killing is strictly in-house and any and all information has to come from the criminal world. However, knowing this also aids the thinking behind underworld murders in the form of disinformation.

If you fill the media and police full of shit prior to a professional killing and just after, you send both groups into an information spin-out.

Also, if you bring in a hit team from outside the mainstream criminal world, then the criminal world itself has to rely on the media or friendly police for 'inside information'. In other words, no one knows anything, but everyone is pretending to know everything.

It's like a game of poker where you pretend to know when you don't and pretend to be confident when you have no right to be.

Acting on information received from insiders who haven't got the faintest idea themselves, media people tell police their secrets, police tell the media their secrets, all of which is based on bullshit from those who don't know. But sometimes it is more sinister, where the disinformation is salted into the mine by those behind the hit in the first place.

I can think of fifteen professional hits in Melbourne that will never be solved, and both the police and the media are busy busting their guts trying to sort out the total shit they have been fed.

Many crimes are hard to commit and harder to conceal. But most murders are easy to solve if handled correctly. Most murders are committed by people in the straight world.

The wife has burned the bacon for the 10,000th time so you stab her in the breast bone. You spend $500,000 on home renovations and your idiot husband gets rounded corners on the granite benches and you hit him on the head with a meat tenderiser.

Then what? No planning. The police come. You end up in a homicide interview room. You tell a few lies but your heart is not in it. You want to confess. You want the nice policeman to tell you that you're not all that bad, that it wasn't your fault. Then, the next thing you're in the dock at the Supreme

Court and you're in the bin for the next ten or fifteen years. That's how it works.

Even most murders involving crooks are the same. Cross words, then a body. Or when the murders are planned, half the time they involve imbeciles. There was the one where they buried the body with lime... but it was the wrong type of lime. And even then the lazy buggers didn't spread it around. They just chucked the bag in the hole.

When they found the body, it was preserved and the bag of lime was still there – sitting on his chest, hard as a rock, because it was the brickies' lime used to make mortar to lay bricks, not quicklime that eats away bodies.

There was also the case of the goose who killed a woman and put her in a drum of chemicals to dissolve the body. Good idea, except the chemical was a preservative. They found the body in mint condition (except she was dead).

I think the crook is now bottling pickled onions in jail, the stupid fat Yank.

That is why homicide squads around Australia have clearance rates of around 90 per cent. Because most murderers are stupid and only marginally smarter than their victims – who must, of course, be even stupider because they ended up dead.

The disinformation must be in place before the gun is even loaded. It's the heat-of-the-moment killings that get solved and that men go to jail for. That, or big-mouth maggots bring themselves and their whole crew undone. Did anyone mention the Russell Street bombing and the Walsh Street murders?

The rule is that, if you shut up and stay shut up, you won't get locked up.

Here's another tip from someone who knows. Stick to the story even if it is a fairy tale. If your fucking mother asks you to tell the real secret, whisper a lie into her ear because sticking with the story is as important as getting rid of the murder weapon.

This is a foolproof tactic because if you don't stick to it you're a fool for giving the police the proof to convict you. After a lifetime − some would say a life sentence − of watching other strategies fail, I've concluded this is the only tactic that works.

You might want to share some secrets with people close to you in the name of business or friendship, but you can never hand over the keys to your heart to anyone because they will surely stab you in it, even if they have to put the knife through your back to do it.

They will be unable to help themselves. Don't you think that Clark Kent wanted to tell someone that he was really Superman? The answer is yes. The hardest thing to keep is a secret and the keepers of secrets are supermen, sometimes super bad men who will go to their graves with their headstones reading 'Rest in Peace Clark Kent'.

People want to talk. The great crims are those who don't need the reputation. Genuine tough men don't have to tell other people how tough they are. They know it and that's all that matters. Beware the quiet man − he can be as deadly as he is rare.

Crims are like anyone else. They want to brag or confide to

mates. But there is no such thing in the underworld as 'mates'. The police have a network of informers who can't wait to pass on any tidbits in exchange for the green light, a blind eye or a sling.

So, if you tell the truth to anyone, you can go to jail. If you tell no one, you have no one to betray you.

That was the trouble with Carl Williams and Melbourne's underworld war. He should have learned from the old Painters and Dockers. Carl was into big statements. He wanted the bodies out there so that everyone knew he did it. He just believed that none of his crew would turn on him. That is why he is a fat wombat that will come out of jail a very old wombat. Or not at all.

Forget the headlines – leave that to the newspapers. He should have moved in quietly, slipped his enemies one by one into the boot and taken them on a one-way ride into the bush. No bodies – no witnesses. Just a few lime funerals and then back to work. But he wanted the grand statement. It backfired big time.

As I said in *Chopper From The Inside*, 'Australia is a big country and shovels are cheap. Victoria may be the garden state but, if you dug it up, you would find a heap of bodies. The garden probably grows so well because of all the blood and bone that has been spread over it.

'If a crook goes missing in Melbourne, chances are he isn't on holiday at Surfers Paradise. Anybody who adds up the numbers over the last hundred years will see I am right. Victoria is the state of the big vanish.'

Is the storyteller himself part of the original thinking behind the longest hit list in Australian criminal history? Good question. I'm glad you've asked. If so, is the storyteller a key player in the massive disinformation programme that smoke screens the men behind it all? Could the storyteller himself be one of the men who helped to draw up the original death list? Good questions, all.

Sure, many of those who have died in the last few years have been enemies of the storyteller. Alphonse Gangitano, Mark, Jason and Lewis Moran have died the most horrible and bloody deaths. Sure, I will not shed crocodile tears or alligator shoes for any of them.

Sure, their deaths have resulted in renewed interests in my books, CDs, films and assorted arms of Chopper Inc, but don't think for a moment that I would assist in letting people leave this mortal place simply for profit and fun. Who do you think I am, some sort of psychopath?

No, no and no. Such a thought would simply be too fantastic to believe. Your legs are being pulled by the old leg puller. And remember, when I pull a leg, sometimes they just come off in my hands. At least, the toes do.

You're so convinced I'm telling you a lie that you can't wait to get to the next page. I'm either one of the best liars in Australia or one of the best storytellers. You be the judge – as long as you don't sit in the Supreme Court.

Let's go back to 1991... three very old and close friends are sitting at a table in a back-street hotel in Collingwood. Three very hated and feared men, they are − outcasts not just from normal everyday society but from a criminal world that neither wants nor trusts them.

Each of the three draws up his own personal hit list of twenty names. One man is to oversee the actual killings, the second to handle the funding and the third to control the disinformation that would smother the biggest death list ever put together in Australian criminal history. Sixty names.

The three men agree it would take years to complete the plan. There could not be wholesale slaughter or even the dimmest police and criminals would be able to see the three as the common denominator.

It was to be done so slowly that the police who began looking at the first murders would be retired before the list was complete. No one would see the connection. You cannot follow the trail if it has grown over.

Revenge is a dish best eaten cold but these three were nothing if not patient. They were prepared to let revenge freeze and thaw out before they were ready to act.

The team knew they would have to use other men to help, and, if needed, kill them to ensure they remained silent. Dead men tell no tales.

They knew it could take up to twenty years. Some would die from natural causes, others would die from the hands of other enemies, but the list would grow and overflow, and end up being anything up to a hundred.

To win a war you can't have a time limit and you have to kill everybody and, naturally, over a twenty-year period, you find yourself planning the murders of men you hadn't known when the list was drawn up.

As I write this, the list is fifteen names down with seven helpers put off as a side issue in the name of silence.

By the time I've finished writing this book, there will have been twenty men crossed off the original list of sixty, with maybe four to six more helpers having to go with them.

Then we will have a list of forty names. Not too many really – you could put them all on one bus. Sixty sounds a bit hard to believe, but, when you read this and learn that there is only forty more to go, it's not such a fantastic tale to believe, after all…

The media will gobble it up as an underworld war. They will never know it is an extermination programme. With any luck, some of those on the list will blame others on the list for some of the deaths and start to kill each other.

It has happened at least twice in the last few years. Saves organisers the effort if they do it to themselves.

When it's all over, the same three original thinkers will meet at the same pub in Collingwood and raise glasses of Irish whiskey and just nod. There will be nothing that will need to be said. That is, if they haven't turned the old pub into a poker machine dump or a coffee shop for trendies.

If they can put a man on the moon, you can kill him when he comes back to earth then you can say, 'Shit, I just shot the man on the moon.' You might get put in a mental hospital but no one will ever believe you enough to send you to jail. That is the beauty of a death list so large. Who is ever going to believe it?

So there it is, the blueprint for a twenty-year gang war hidden by a sea of bullshit, put together by the greatest criminal psychologist in the game, funded by cocaine dollars and heroin money handed over willingly by the new style of young Turks (or should that be Lebanese Tony?) waiting to take over a criminal world and drug empire still ruled by men from the 1970s. Oh, I've forgotten the meth-amphetamine money.

The young drug dealers knew that, if the dinosaurs of the criminal world fought, then the ants may rule. But they didn't for a moment know the size of the plans.

The three original thinkers didn't take a penny of this cash. Every cent was spent on outside help, arms, ammo, travel, accommodation, logistic support, intelligence and counter-intelligence. Spies and networks of spies, all working for controllers on a need-to-know basis within the various enemy camps.

It is the greatest military criminal operation ever launched in Australian criminal history.

Why, you ask? To which the answer is: For the best reason of all… Why not?

You can turn a lie into the truth within a month. Police investigations are launched on the basis of one body and one lie. They then proceed to go no place. Into the valley of the blind and in any war it is always good to pop off a few non-event bastards who have nothing to do with anything other than the fact that they knew a few of the real targets.It is a totally one-sided war, but it must appear to look like a gang war. In a gang war, both sides know who they are up against but, in this war, only one side is getting hit by an enemy they cannot see and do not know.

It creates paranoia and, in some cases, friends turn on friends and kill each other... It's like Dr Frankenstein's monster: once something is created, it is very hard to control it. The whole thing can take on a life of its own, leaving the original thinkers to sit and wonder about it all. Wonder or marvel at the monster they created and. But, like Dr Frankenstein, the creators must be aware that the monster can turn on them at any time.

So the best idea is to quietly withdraw, watch and wait and simply allow the game to continue, directing play from time to time with a good hit or two and a few good lies just to keep the players interested.

Fantastic, isn't it? Quite simply outrageous and truly unbelievable. However, where are the revenge killings, where are the arrests and convictions. There are none. War, what war?

The police and the media all sense they are watching the biggest gang war in Australian criminal history but they can't quite understand the logic of it. And, for the police and the media, if it doesn't make sense, they simply can't accept it. They look at each death in isolation or as a small group – a spate of murders over months or a couple of years. None look at all of them. They can't see the big picture, but only because no one looks.

For the original thinkers, it is a game of chess and they are the masters. They will either win the game or destroy the whole criminal structure as it stands. It is as simple as that. Either way they win.

You can believe this or disregard it as nonsense. I personally don't give a shit. I'm Mark 'Chopper' Read. I've written numerous bestsellers and had a movie made about my life. Do you really think I give a shit who believes me or not? If you don't, you can always buy a newspaper and read how the media know all and claim that police know who did this, that and the other and are hoping for an early arrest. And they reckon I'm the one who's pulling people's legs.

I can write it all down in the comic knowledge that none of you will believe a word I'm writing. The only safe way to tell the truth is when you know people are convinced you're lying.

Like when I told the police I killed Sammy the Turk, they just didn't believe me. Sammy did. But, sadly, he was in no condition to corroborate my story.

It was the confession and the story that went with it and the fact that police did not act on a confession that ultimately helped the jury come to the wise decision that I was not guilty of murder.

But then, what would I know; after all, I am the greatest liar on earth. Would I tell anyone the truth?

So a wall of disbelief protects this whole story. Don't you think these tactics have ever been used before? Hitler once said, 'The greater the lie, the more people will believe it.' Do you think that the truth is a weapon ever used in war?

John F Kennedy. Martin Luther King. Do you really believe that disinformation wasn't the greatest weapon used before and after their deaths? The list goes on and on.

Just read history, military history, political history, any sort of history. The people either don't want to, or simply will not, believe the truth, so a lie must be created for them and, when a writer writes about lies, how can he ever be sued or charged for telling the truth?

I feel I sit here writing this with a certain legal safety. I will repeat, you can either believe it or not, I will not confirm nor will I deny. You be the jury.

Tears mean nothing when they are insincere. Even real tears can conceal a murderer. As you know, the deep thinkers who put Mad Charlie off still miss him greatly, but sometimes things have to be done. The sentimental gangster will die or spend his life in jail. Only the cool heads and the cold-hearted survive…

There is an old saying that property makes cowards of us all. It's true, even in the criminal world. The up-and-coming gangster is the most dangerous because he has nothing to lose. Once he has made a mark, settled down with a family and begun raking in the cash, he is terrified. Frightened someone will target him, take his spot, take his money, tell the cops and ruin his party. Most of the time he is right.

In that world, you can't afford to let a man live just because he might be a good bloke and might not be an informer. Might not means that he also might be. Only death will make sure he isn't. Simple as that. You are the Weakest Link – bang! It takes the guess out of the guessing game.

It is also true that most of the top drug criminals in Melbourne and Sydney have some form of relationship with some police. So it is not hard to convince a paranoid drug boss that so-and-so is an informer because he thinks to himself, 'Well, I've got my police that I talk to, why should he be the odd man out?'

The fire is already set, you just have to find the right match. It's simply a matter of knowing thy enemy and knowing him very well. Are you seeing now how the original list of sixty men to be killed over a fifteen- to twenty-year period wasn't really so far-fetched at all?

Think of the murders that remain unsolved. Freddie the Frog lost half his head in the docks back in the 1950s. His mate, Big Normie, fell out of the sky not long after. The Ferret went swimming in his Valiant. It wasn't roadworthy, let alone seaworthy. Painters and Dockers painted themselves into dark corners, drug dealers went on missing lists and crooks retired into shallow graves. The police didn't try too hard. Many thought the crims got their right whack.

The coppers, meanwhile, were trying to solve murders of innocent people. When they deal with crims who either won't talk or talk bullshit, they lose interest pretty quickly.

Let us now return to 12 November 1979, and a man by the name of Raymond Patrick Chuck, head of the crew that carried out the Great Bookie Robbery on the Victorian Club in Queen Street on 26 April 1976. The papers said between $1 million and $12 million was believed taken. I have always believed it was $6 million but some very good judges, who know about how much bookies were holding and how much they owed, calculate that it was less than that.

In any case, it was still plenty of money for those days, so who's counting?

Ray Chuck was shot dead as he was escorted through the Melbourne Magistrates' Court. The rumours put about were that the late criminal gang leader and standover merchant Brian Kane pulled the trigger as a payback for the death of his brother, Leslie Herbert Kane.

Whispers were then heard that professional hitman Christopher Dale Flannery, nicknamed 'Rent-A-Kill', did the job, setting in place probably the greatest disinformation campaign ever conceived. If Ray Chuck was killed by Flannery, then the answer to who killed Flannery is too fucking easy.

Who was Ray Chuck's best friend in the world? I won't name him, as he is still alive and remains one of the best crooks in Australia. He isn't a bad bloke at all and certainly doesn't deserve to do a life sentence over a maggot like Flannery.

To add punch to the party, you had all these razzle-dazzle Sydney gangsters either bragging that they shot Flannery or that they knew who did. So the disinformation campaign put in place to protect the true identity of the man who did kill Flannery wasn't hard, but it was massive, and went on for years.

It's hard to come back and say, 'Oh, by the way, to prove my point on the psychology of criminal gang warfare, fear and the sheer power of disinformation, I'd now like to confess that I invented 90 per cent of the crap people now believe to be fact surrounding the Flannery case.' That would be stupid, wouldn't it?

Now, it is true that the team carrying out the inquest into the death of sad old Chris did come down to Risdon Prison in sleepy Tassie to have a chat with me. They asked me a great number of questions. I can understand why they would want my views on such a serious matter. After all, with due modesty, I do possess the greatest criminal mind of any (living) underworld identity. Which proves mainly that there aren't that many heavy thinkers in criminal ranks.

Anyway, so they rocked down for a chat. I spoke for a great deal of time. They listened, took more notes and nodded gravely. I nodded gravely. They asked more questions and took more notes. Each one of them got more than a grand a day for asking questions. I got bugger-all for answering them. They went back to their five-star hotels to mull over what I had said with the help of a cheeky Pinot and a local lobster. I had rissoles for tea washed down with some prison hooch. You work it out.

They seemed happy. I was happy. Did I feed them some disinformation? Perish the thought. As a law-abiding citizen – not – I did my best to help, but no one (including me) has done a day's jail over Chris, who, rumour suggests, may have given a white pointer shocking heartburn.

I know of several investigations, still unsolved, where police scientific investigators mistook a gunshot wound from a .22-calibre magnum handgun as that of a 38-calibre.

The slug passed straight through the body and was never found, so the whole homicide squad is busy, busy, busy sorting out the disinformation on murders they will never solve, beginning with scientific evidence, sending the investigators in search of the wrong weapon. How do I know that? Maybe I made it up, or maybe I know the killer. Maybe I know the killer very well.

I won't start on police scientific investigators. Remember the Azaria Chamberlain case. Blood spots, which turned out to be paint spots when they enter the courtroom. It's a nice trip up the yellow brick road.

Scientific evidence doesn't have to be 100 per cent spot-on any more. The introduction of DNA evidence means that all that is needed now is to be pretty close, not 100 per cent. But a fair chance and that's that, you're guilty.

Add that crap to police evidence based on several years of disinformation along with police ballistic experts who can't tell a .22-calibre magnum head wound from the head wound of a .38. I can think of several fellows, although very guilty of a hundred other unsolved crimes, who didn't do the ones they are in prison for. Quite comic really, in a poetic justice sort of way. Life all seems to equal itself out in the end. Just ask Alphonse. His equalled itself out a little earlier than he'd hoped. Never mind, if he believed in reincarnation, perhaps he'll get a longer tour of duty next time.

But I'm getting off the track.

Remember Victor Frederick Allard, a former Painter and Docker turned drug dealer? He was shot to death in February 1979, in Fitzroy Street, St Kilda. And Michael Ebert, who was shot to death on 17 April 1980, outside a brothel off Rathdowne Street, Carlton? Both unsolved. Police and media all think they know the answer, but, if they know so fucking much, then how come no arrests or convictions?

Did Shane Goodfellow really die of a drug overdose in 1992 or was it a hotshot murder? The same with Tony MacNamara – but, again, I digress. I tend to do this.

> *'Mentally speaking, it's pretty hard to pull your socks up*
> *when you're only wearing fucking thongs.'*
> FRANKIE WAGHORN – H DIVISION LEGEND
> AND THE HARDEST PUNCHER IN THE
> UNDERWORLD.

I'm not the only one to use the psychology of fear or to weave a web of disinformation to conceal the truth.

Take the case of Santo Ippolito in December 1991. Santo was bashed to death in his home in Springvale. Case unsolved. Disinformation claimed within underworld circles that a member of my crew hired through me was paid to do it. I've never heard of the bloke in my life. And if I had heard of him I wouldn't tell you. I didn't get all this way to lag myself back into jail. Twenty-four years is enough for anyone.

The case of Vietnamese drug dealer Quock Cuong Dwong, killed on 30 January 1992. The story put out was that it was a torture job again. Again, baseless rumours that members of my old crew were close to the scene. There was even one yarn that had me actually involved. Again, never heard of the bloke. I am offended by these slanders against me.

But the best was when the dagos killed Rocco Medici and his brother Giuseppe Furina and dumped them in the Murrumbidgee River after cutting their ears off. I'm unsure of the date, but it was back in the Eighties and it may have been 5 May 1984, at a spooky guess.

It was during the height of the Pentridge Overcoat Gang War and a membership drive of the Van Gogh club, which is far more exclusive than the Melbourne Club. Members of my crew, on the outside, were rumoured to have been paid by the Italians to carry out the murders, and the ears was a comic touch. A sort of Van Gogh signature.

In all of the history of the Italian criminal culture, ear cutting has never been a part of the play. That bit of disinformation lasted about two days until a few wogs were told that the next lot of ears to come off would be their own. End of disinformation programme, but they are still unsolved murders.

And, now, if I may quote myself from an earlier work regarding these matters:

'If you have a dead body in the bottom of your swimming

pool and the police are on their way over to interview you about a missing wristwatch, then the only thing you can do is toss dirt into the pool and muddy the water. What people can't see they won't worry about. The police may remark on your dirty swimming pool but, for the time being, that's it until the next move, which is hopefully out of the fucking swimming pool.'

To which I would add a thought from Sherlock Holmes:

'Ninety per cent of all criminal cases solved are the direct result of information received. The remaining ten per cent belong to the investigating criminal detective and nine per cent of those cases are bungled by forensic fools. The impossible one per cent are totally unsolvable. The per cent remaining is then handed to us, my dear Watson.'

What the media, police, writers and movie directors call the underworld they never truly understand. The logic is to ignore logic, which means you have to unlearn what you have been taught.

People, including police, think too much. They start by saying, 'If I was the crook, I would have done this.' They give most crooks too much credit for planning and logic. Dennis Allen shot a bloke for putting the wrong record on in his lounge room. Work that out – he would have been a shocking DJ.

We had a war in jail because I was alleged to have eaten too many sausages, a foul piece of slander indeed – although I must say they were yummy.

Nothing makes sense and, when you understand that, everything falls into place. There is no logic in shooting someone outside a crowded nightclub, cutting your ears off and baseball-batting various fat wombats in front of witnesses. But, believe me, it happens.

There is no master plan, just a sea of human filth trying to get to the surface for a breath of pure air. I have known of crims on their way to a million-dollar heroin deal who have shoplifted a coat on the way. If they had been caught, the deal would have gone sour. Why did they do it? Because they could.

Many years ago, a very well-known radio type, later to become a TV personality, was debating the rape issue on talkback radio with a high-profile lady in the women's movement. She stopped him dead by saying, 'Well, it's a waste of my time debating this point with you. You have never been raped – I have.'

The next day, the radio personality shocked his listeners by breaking down and tearfully confessing that he had been the victim of sexual molestation as a child at the hands of his uncle. Game, set and match to him. He had not only won the debate but gained the sympathy of a whole new audience.

The only evidence that what he said was true was his own word. But why would a man say such a thing if it weren't true? Why indeed! Think of the psychological advantage. Another famous personality comes out and confesses to being homosexual, then writes a bestseller on the topic. The truth was he was really straight and just pretending to be gay.

I have shot a few and a few have died – big deal. But, in reality, Chopper Read was a less-than-average criminal who used greater-than-average violence for less-than-average money. But Chopper Read could spin a greater-than-above-average story and he could get people laughing. I'm a self-made man with an unmade face and an unfilled grave. It has now reached the stage that fact can no longer be separated from fiction.

That's what a true legend is. A legend is a myth. It is a lie welded together with the truth and used as a cosh to beat the unsuspecting around the head. I've done it and now I'm telling you, believe nothing except what you yourself believe to be true while all the time being aware that you could be wrong.

I will take a little mental rest now. My doctor warned me not to get into these spinouts as I start to waffle and I suspect I'm starting to rave a little. Then again, sometimes the truth of a situation can be clearly seen only after talking to a total mental case.

I must go and find one.

Who created Chopper Read? Well, first of all, I did it myself with some big help of the police. Then, of course, the media got in for its chop, if you know what I mean. Chopper Read's image is largely a media-created package. A virtual reality, multi-media package with no ears and a heap of tattoos, tied up in a bow…

Chopper Read is who and what you think he is because he told you he is. Others have confirmed my reality because I told them it was so. Maybe I don't exist at all. How many of you have seen me in the flesh? Only a few dozen people of the hundreds of thousands who have read the books and seen the movie.

An enemy of your enemy is a friend. It's been true for thousands of years, and will be for thousands more.

Alex Tsakmakis was a millionaire and a killer. He chucked a professional runner named Bruce Walker in the bay in 1978. Walker was a good runner but not much of a swimmer, which was no surprise given that he was trussed up in chicken wire at the time.

Tsakmakis then set fire to Barry Robert Quinn in Jika Jika in 1984. Quinn had baited him about his girlfriend. It was a dumb move by Bazza. Alex squirted him with glue and then flicked matches at Barry. Whoosh! Barry was burned alive. Not a good way to go. And the scorched smell was around for days.

There was a death notice the next day that was supposed to come from Alex saying, 'Sorry, we always stuck together.' Call me a cynic but I reckon there was a touch of 'blue' humour in that one.

I stabbed Alex in the neck once while he was reading the *Financial Review* in the exercise yard, the pretentious bastard. He wasn't too tough when he was screaming around with blood pissing out where his collar used to be. He always was a pain in the neck.

I was kicked out of the section for that, which I thought was a bit harsh so I wrote to the Classo Board:

Dear Classo Board,

I would very much like to go back into the same yard as Alex Tsakmakis, I like him and I get on very well with him. Unfortunately, I took a turn for the worse today, and very nearly made a fatal mistake. I am very sorry for this, the wrong thing was said at the wrong time. I was worried and upset about another matter and Alex said something to me that upset me for a moment.

I was in the wrong, by taking the action that I did. I'm sorry if you do not want to put me back into the yard with Alex, I will understand your action, but nevertheless I have no plans to harm Alex and I do not believe he has a plan to harm me in any way. I know that you all believe me to be a smiling mad man, and I have done nothing to prove you wrong. If you do not put me and Alex back together again, then what? Problems, problems, problems. I feel that I should give some form of explanation re my actions towards Alex Tsakmakis.

I was in a very sad mood after a visit with my father. I had been let down badly by a newspaperman who had for the last year claimed to be writing a book about me. My father plans to go down to Tassie in four years time, leaving me here on my own.

I know that I will rot in this Division forever and a day. I am bored stiff and I am slowly going out of my mind in this place. I'm doing a seventeen-and-a-half-year sentence over a man who betrayed me and, from my point of view, my life is hopeless, and I have nothing in the world to lose…

Once again, I would like to go back with Alex Tsakmakis.
Question. Why is it that you always put me in spots where I
have nothing to lose and then you wonder why I crack up now
and again? Why don't you try doing me a good turn instead
of a bad turn and you would find out that I would never let
you down.

If I was a paranoid person, I could easily believe that you
have placed me in spots where you knew that sooner or later
blood would flow, and my body, or someone else's, would be
carried out in a bag.

(As for the newspaperman who said he was writing a book
about me. I wonder how he feels now. You had your
chance, you fool.)

Eventually, we were placed back in the one division.

After that, Alex and I became allies, even though he hated
me. We had another dangerous opponent so we stuck
together. Remember, the enemy of my enemy is my friend.

But, much later, after Russell Street bomber Craig Minogue
joined the division, I heard that Alex had put a $7000 contract
out on me. Now, that was a lot of money inside – for that sort
of cash I would nearly have done it myself.

I was saddened. Our alliance was over – although Alex
didn't know it. He came to me with the plan to kill big
Craig. He had a leather punch spike he wanted to drive into
Craig's brain.

I warned Fatty Minogue about the attack. The big fella was

116

to lose so much weight he was called Slim. Should have been called Jenny Craig Minogue.

When Alex went into the yard, Craig was waiting with a couple of gym weights in a pillow case. He wasn't looking for a workout. He swung them around and turned Alex's brains to mashed potato.

I sat in my cell having a smoke. Sometimes generals don't have to fire the bullets, just move in the troops.

Slim was my friend. We both are still alive. Alex is dead. That's how it works.

Churchill and Stalin. The Poms had no time for the Frogs, and vice versa, but they fought together in two world wars against the Hun. Enough lessons from the past.

If you don't get it by now, pay for cable TV and watch the history channel.

Billy the Texan Longley once said to me that I was without a shadow of a doubt the greatest psychological manipulator of the media in Australian criminal history, but the same people dismiss me as not much of a crook compared to their great selves, of course.

My idea of a successful criminal isn't much different from a successful anything else: someone who ends up with wealth, power, fame and long life.

Few crooks gain power, very few gain fame and even fewer gain long life. So a crook who has gained wealth, power, fame and long life is the winner – no contest.

Good crooks are never known. They have power and money without the fame. Serial killers get the fame with no power and no money and, usually, a lifetime behind bars. Violent criminals have a certain power, but only until they lose their strength, then they either reform or die. Some just get out of jail and become hairdressers like William John O'Meally.

I had fame, power and not much money. I can tell you that writing about crime is a hell of a lot better than committing it. That's why crime reporters tend to live longer than the criminals they write about. Except if they die of mixed grill and beer poisoning.

I'm a forward thinker. I'm not so worried about today's opinion but of tomorrow's and I suspect new generations will view this no-eared freak with a kinder heart than the mice who roar at me today. History has shown us that.

Speaking of mice, one of Beethoven's critics from the media, a name I forget, contacted a former Victorian Police Detective Inspector who, in turn, rang me. As a favour to the former inspector I rang the mouse, or mousette. She was doing an article on me, the movie and so on. I tried to explain that all the money that was due to me from the movie had already been signed over to a children's hospital cancer foundation, but she didn't want to know this as the fact that I'd already given the movie money away to charity flew in the face of her 'why criminals make money from crime' articles. Again, it's an example of how the truth is never believed. People would rather believe the lie than the truth.

All she wanted was a black story and so she didn't want a white answer. She only wanted the legend, the myth and the lie – and anything that wavered from what she had already planned on writing was, to her, a lie. She intended to turn her version into reality by printing it, then it would become the 'truth'. That is, the truth to a vast number of her unsuspecting readers.

I was too polite to mention that the only person making any money at the time was her. I wasn't being paid for the interview and she was getting plenty. I've seen a lot of hypocrisy and dishonesty and a lot of rackets in my time, but I've never seen more hypocrisy and dishonesty than there is in the media racket. They're geniuses at it.

There are basically three sorts of crime. Unorganised Crime – lawless activity by individuals; Disorganised Crime – lawless activity by gangs; and Organised Crime – lawless activity by gangs, crews, teams, cartels, syndicates, call them what you will.

The Mafia is a continuing, never-ending tree of criminal conspiracy to gain economic power via physical force and private corruption. It is kept alive with the falling leaf attitude. Each member is only a leaf, the roots of the tree are in place and so is the trunk. The leaves that do or don't blow off (or get blown away) won't affect the health of the tree itself. I've chainsawed big trees down and watched new trees grow ten metres away from the stump: new trees that sprang from the old tree's original root system.

Any organised criminal group that has not been cut down within its first generation of life will never be cut down, as the root system after the first generation has taken hold. Any group that can trace its roots back 300 years or even thirty years is cemented in place.

Leaves may fall but the tree will remain. Any police or media remark to the contrary is flapdoodle, pure and simple. We should also remember that some police and the (very) odd journalist has been a member of a crime family or two.

I'm not saying that criminal activity is a myth or nonsense, it is all very real, dangerous and deadly serious, be it unorganised, disorganised or highly organised or spur-of-the-moment thoughtless madness.

You are just as dead if you are shot by some idiot with a crime fantasy and a stolen .22 pea rifle as you are if you are blown away by a marksman hired by a crime cartel using a state-of-the-art, high-powered sniper rifle that can take out a buffalo at two miles.

What I'm saying is that this psychology of fear is an important tool used at all levels of criminal activity and, one day, the crime fighters and people who report on crime will come to understand this tactic.

I feel at times the police and the various news media do to a certain agree understand the fear myth I've outlined and they themselves use this very tactic to frighten governments via the general public.

Budget funding relies heavily on public demand for more police to fight serious crime. The news media is not a public charity – the more the media can frighten the public, the more newspapers they can sell and viewers they can attract.

TV news and current affairs and crime documentaries rely heavily on this same psychology. The old Chinese proverb of killing one to scare ten thousand is very true and much used by all parties involved: cops, robbers, reporters and the humble spectator.

They shiver in fright and vote with their minds, hearts and wallets to protect themselves from a monster that is largely a phantom of disinformation.

People fear what they don't understand and keeping the general public in a state of semi-ignorance is an important tool in the battle plans of both the good guys and the bad guys.

We work together to keep the square-heads in the dark. Politicians win, because they get votes from being tough on crime; coppers win, because they get more money and influence; and the media wins because they have more stories to tell and sell. The crooks win, in a way, because they become more feared.

Know this and believe it because the bloke writing this has mastered and used this very tool for well over twenty years. For once, the humble reader is being invited to look behind a closely guarded and secret door only to find the monster is mostly imagination. It is all a Hollywood production.

There is no one in the audience... we are all up on the stage.

CHAPTER 4

CHOPPER ON...

THE ART OF VIOLENCE AND THE LIFE OF CRIME

*It's called literary licence, and it's a lot easier
to get than a gun licence*

Apart from Irish whiskey, good cigars, Pontiac motor cars
and a pistol-grip baby .410 shotgun with solid load shells,
what I love most is kidnapping smartarse gangsters and
taking their money. To the human filth I have bashed, belted,
iron-barred, axed, shot, stabbed, knee-capped, set on fire
and driven to their graves, I can only quote from the motto
of the French Foreign Legion, 'Je Ne Regrette Rien'...
I REGRET NOTHING.

I was walking to the shops when the would-be hitman got
me. The moral is simple: never go to the shops without your
recyclable bags – or your gun.

Strange as it may seem, I have never considered myself a murderer, because they all had it coming. Most of them came under the heading of tactical necessities. All of them were killers and violent crims, so big deal.

Just a point of interest, every man that I have shot or stabbed who lived looked up at me like a beaten puppy and asked, 'Why?' Before a man dies, his last word always seems to be 'No'.

Men from certain ethnic groups cry and scream and go to their deaths like screaming females, crying, 'No, No, No.'

The smell when you put a blowtorch to someone's feet is hard to describe. It is a cross between burned hair and roast pork.

None of the people I've killed were innocent, normal or average nine-to-five working types: they were all drug dealers, hoons, pimps, crime figures and killers. I doubt whether any of them was a virgin as far as death and murder were concerned. Some of them had killed plenty in the drug world with a needle.

They say there are no atheists on foxholes, and I have stood at the edge of the grave for most of my life. It is hard for me not to wonder, at times, why I am still alive. How have I continued to escape death in every life and death situation?

I was the victim of schoolyard bullies five days a week. I grew up to hate bullies. I guess that's why I took such delight in belting the hell out of the so-called 'tough guys' when I grew up. I was violent, but not a bully. Everyone I've ever moved against has been a bullyboy, a two-bob tough guy.

Most of the truly violent men I've known in my life have been the victims of school bullies and violence in the home.

'A general bit of shooting makes you forget your troubles and take the mind off the cost of living.'

'Men who are forced to kill or be killed in the criminal world are another story, as what they do isn't real murder. It is simply the way it is and the way it has to go… kill or be killed is not murder in my book.'

'Curly Bill once rode 300 miles to kill three men in the Red Dog Saloon. I myself would have taken a taxi. Which brings me to a matter of financial concern. If you were a professional killer, could you write off cab fares like that as a tax deduction? Surely a hitman could claim guns, bullets and suchlike as business expenses. It seems only fair.'

'When the man from the city robs you, he will do it with a gun to your head or a blade at your throat and have the manners to wear a mask, whereas the man from the bush will do it with a firm handshake and a warm smile.'

'It seems to me that terrorism is a weapon of anger and not of intelligence.'

It is interesting that most gunmen, myself included, soon learn to take an interest in matters medical. The human body is a tough thing and, if you want to fix it, like a doctor, or hurt it, like a toe-cutter, you have to know what you are doing. Each profession takes skill, although it is a little hard to bulk bill as a standover man.

When I shot Chris Liapas in Footscray, I used a Beretta .32-calibre automatic. The bullet went in his guts and the doctors found it in his underpants when he got to hospital. It had passed out his bottom. Amazing.

I shot another bloke in Carlton in the neck with a .22-calibre revolver. He coughed the slug up and spat it out as he ran away. Talk about spitting chips.

'I know I talk about guns a lot, but I get pleasure from them. They are my tools of trade, but they are also my hobby. I must confess, although it is not much of a secret, that I do enjoy shooting a total arse-wipe.'

'To me, it is a game and, if you are caught, then it is no use howling and pretending that you are some whiter-than-white saint who has never done the wrong thing.

'Many crims eventually convince themselves that they didn't do it, even when they are caught with the smoking gun in their hands and there are a hundred witnesses prepared to swear that they saw the bloke pull the trigger.

'I am not like that. If I did it and I am caught, then it's a fair cop and you do the time without complaining.'

'The average crook involved in these criminal war situations has no flair or imagination. If they are prepared to listen and follow my advice, I'll help.

'I love a good criminal war or battle situation and I am only ever consulted on matters of violence and death.'

'But, in the true world of criminal "bang bang you're dead" violence, it doesn't matter how well you can fight or play footy. If your number comes up, you are off tap and that is that. Dead as a bloody mackerel, no questions asked.'

'I mean, getting stabbed, shot, bashed, verballed, slandered, abused, betrayed while being investigated by your own side while upholding law and order and the good of the community… this is meant to be a career?'

'You can't complain that you only pulled your weapon out to frighten the policeman and that you weren't really going to use it. If you pull a weapon out on someone to scare them, then you stand a bloody good chance of scaring them into blowing your bloody head off.

'Silly bastards. The more crims and nutters who get blown away by police and the more police who get blown away by the crims and nutters, the more paranoid and frightened both sides become.

'So welcome to America. It's what Australia wanted, to copy America. But, whereas cats have nine lives, copy cats get only one.'

It is my own personal opinion that the Victoria Police is the most blood-soaked body of men and women in Australian law-enforcement history.

They have been baptised in a sea of their own blood, along with the blood and guts of those who went up against them.

'All this needless violence is caused by too much television, if you ask me. Bloody Aussie land is going mad, and in my opinion the whole bloomin' country could do with a valium, a good cup of tea and a nice lie down.'

'My enemies have fallen, weakened and run because they have placed more importance on their own lives than I did. Don't misunderstand, I don't want to die. I want to live as long as God allows. But I don't fear death. As long as my death has a certain amount of style, flair and dash involved, I don't mind.'

'I will never surrender. I will fight on in the face of unbeatable odds. I simply will not plead guilty to a crime that I simply did not do. Why should I? Would you? I think not. So why should I be forced to plead guilty on a matter I didn't do just because I am a career criminal.'

'Once the blood starts flying, politics and talk won't solve anything.'

'What I lack in the finer points of fisticuffs I make up for in violence.'

'You don't get a reputation like mine for being a nice guy.'

'I have grown to despise and loathe the mainstream criminal population, for they are nothing but weak-gutted mice.'

'If you get to the frontline of a war, you can be the safest.'

'Now the crims are feeding off each other. They have become cannibals. The dope dealers are all robbing each other, the bank robbers are robbing each other, the massage parlours are standing over each other, the nightclub owners are standing over and robbing each other.'

'If people want fair play, let them join a cricket club. A street fight is a no-holds-barred, anything-goes battle between two men or ten men. Anything can be used, from a slap on the face with a wet tea towel to a meat axe through the brain. Mainly fists, feet, knees and head butts are used, if a heavy object is not close to hand.'

'But guts without guns in my world can be fatal.'

'It now appears to me that I can only trust someone when I have a loaded gun stuck in their mouth. Although, of course, it is rude to speak with one's mouth full.'

'One thing I want to make very clear as a criminal, I am in a class that is no threat whatsoever to Mr and Mrs Average. The normal honest person has nothing to fear from me. Chopper Read won't break into your home, he won't pinch your TV, video or purse. He won't rape your daughter, wife, sister or granny. He won't pinch your car, rob your bank, café or off-licence. No, I am not in an area of crime that would personally touch the lives of the ordinary individual.

'I am not even in an area of crime that will touch the ordinary criminal.

'I am, or was, in a league alone, working in a specialised area of crime that the ordinary type of criminal only comes into contact with in his nightmares.'

'I know my not guilty plea is a fart in the face of a thunderstorm.'

'I have been known to take wounded men to hospital but I don't take dead men to the morgue.'

'He looked quite surprised when I pulled out my trusty meat cleaver and slammed it down on the bar.'

'To me violence was an art, and I was the artist.'

'A nice bit of sharp pain clears the mind and cleanses the soul. I personally see the lash as a bloody good character builder. If you can't hang them, lash them and, if you can't lash them, bash them.'

'The criminal world is populated by three basic types – social spastics, mental retards and brain-dead junkies. There is also a smattering of freaks and flukes.

'If you are a social spastic, a mental retard or a brain-dead junkie, or even a freak, and you haven't been caught or jailed, then you are definitely a fluke.'

'Death never brawls in the street. Death never has to throw a punch. Death only smiles, puts his hand inside his coat and says in a quiet voice, "Excuse me, mate, I didn't quite hear that. Were you talking to me?"

'Men found blown away in car parks have generally been stupid enough to invite death outside for a fist fight.

'Death never has to raise his voice or his fist in anger, the most polite and well-mannered gent you will ever meet in the world is the hangman.'

'Lesson: don't ever question the impact of a gun at a criminal arms deal. Not unless you have tin legs, anyway.'

'The professional policeman and the professional criminal: there is not a lot to separate them.'

I saw a young girl, she looked about 13, wearing a short, white summer frock with white Roman sandals. She had lovely blonde hair and was about five foot. She would have looked very pretty if it wasn't for the fact she was sobbing, and had tears and a smattering of blood down her face.

I asked her what was the matter and she told me that Turkish George had bashed her. I asked her why and she told me, this little schoolgirl, that she was using smack and doing dirty deeds at the weekend to pay for it. She had some personal pride and wouldn't do some of the dirty deeds that Turkish George wanted her to do. She said she was only a part-time user and didn't have a habit.

She pointed out Turkish George, then I asked her whether she knew me. She said she didn't. I then asked her if she had heard of Chopper Read. She said she had heard the name in the street.

I said, 'I am Chopper Read... and you are going to run on home and never show your face in St Kilda again.'

She promised me she would clear out, and left.

I walked up the street a bit and saw Turkish George sitting in the passenger side of a P76 car with the door open, talking to some fat-arsed pro.

I had a pair of pliers. There is an art to using a pair of pliers in a street fight, but I won't go into that. I punched approximately 30 puncture wounds into the Turk's face and nearly blinded him – and I did it all in broad daylight while two uniformed police sat twenty feet away in a police car, eating hamburgers.

When Turkish George was a limp, bleeding mess in the gutter, I said to the cops, 'Let's go.'

They handcuffed me and I was in the back of the police car when the ambulance arrived to take Turkish George away.

I was released on bail on my own reconnaissance after

being charged with grievous bodily harm. It appears that the police hated Turkish George and thought his injuries were poetic justice. At my trial, the magistrate asked if there was anything I wanted to say. I said, 'Yes, I am only sorry I didn't blind the bastard completely.'

I pleaded guilty, and got only two years. Big deal.

I was told later in jail by a junkie who knew St Kilda well that the little blonde girl didn't return to Fitzroy Street. It was well worth two years.

'An enemy can cripple itself with its own fear.'

'Everyone fears the unknown; everyone gets a jump in their hearts out of a bump in the night. Everybody wants to go to heaven but nobody wants to die first.'

'Then, through the use of personal contact via the telephone or even a nice card or flowers, you can turn up the heat. Bumping into their old mother with a warm smile and a hello, and asking her to pass on your regards to Sonny Boy. Paranoia and fear combine to create an almost crippled mental state. The war at that stage has been won, and I haven't left my lounge chair.

'The actual physical part of this form of combat via a death or act of violence is a small part. It is the very last move on the chessboard. I play this game over a period of time to create the maximum tension and stress.'

'As a wise man once said, "Kill one, scare one thousand." Even the strong and strong-minded can fall victim, as they can't realise it is happening to them. They can't separate the mind game from the reality. The psychology of fear.'

'Using fear correctly is a skill, even an art. Its correct use, I believe, is to instil fear in your targets with a wink and a smile – using courtesy and a friendly, polite attitude… After all, as our mothers taught us, a spoonful of sugar helps the medicine go down.'

'I have outlined the theory before that lust attacks the groin first, the brain second and then the heart. Love attacks the heart first, the brain second and then the groin. Fear attacks only the brain, then cripples every other part of the body.'

'Love, lust and hate are the basic emotions and feelings that the average person deals with. Fear is not something the average person has to confront or even wishes to confront in an average lifetime. So using fear and controlling it is not something that the average person has to do. The basic fear that sits in all men's hearts is that each man knows himself. Despite the opinions of others, every man is aware that deep down he is not as good as others think, and that, one day, that may be exposed.'

'Fear is a phantom, a puff of smoke that can be blown into the eyes to cloud the mind and thoughts. It can destroy logic and reason if you do not understand it. How true is the saying "We have nothing to fear but fear itself".'

When I first picked up a handgun (a .32-calibre revolver), my dad, who served twenty-four years in the army, put a beer bottle at my feet and told me to try to hit it. And aiming at the bottle from a standing position, I missed it three shots in a row. My dad then taught me to sight a firearm at an old fridge door at an army firing range. He would draw an X on the fridge door with a black marker and then at a distance of thirty paces he would tell me to take aim and fire.

I'd miss the target by at least a foot, which wasn't too bad for a fifteen-year old.

Then he told me to move my barrel aim two inches to the right and an inch above the target, and I hit the cross. My dad told me that you always miss the first shot. Then you have to sight the gun in. Generally, you have to move your aim two inches to the right and one inch above at a distance of thirty paces.

Then he taught me to fire a single-action handgun. Remember the old Wild West movies when Billy The Kid would pull out his Colt .45 single action and hold his trigger finger against the trigger and then fan the hammer back across the hammer with the other hand? That wasn't for show. That is the only way to fire a single-action handgun with speed, as you have to pull the hammer back after each shot. But, if you have one hand holding the trigger down and the other hand fanning the hammer back, you can discharge the firearm with some speed, as fast as a double-action or even faster.

So, learning to shoot was quality time for Dad and me. Sure he didn't help me with schoolwork but as it turned out this was the best homework I could do considering the line of work I ended up in.

Being taught to use a handgun by my dad at a young age put me in good stead on the streets of Melbourne when gunplay was involved. I've been questioned thirty-three times for non-fatal shootings in Melbourne, and they all got to hospital. I didn't do them all (about eleven were down to me) but they were all leg and lower-stomach wounds — none of them fatal shots and all at a goodly distance of up to twenty or thirty paces.

I'd gladly face any gunman in Melbourne at a distance of thirty paces, in the full knowledge of how to sight a small-calibre weapon in. I could hit you in the kneecap at a distance of six metres and any police officer who used the firing range regularly could tell you that is good shooting. I could take out car tyres at a distance of ten metres as they speed past at 80 kph. That's good shooting if I say so myself. And I do.

I shot a stubbie beer bottle out of Trent Anthony's hand for a TV shoot in Tassie with a semi-auto Ruger thirty-shot .22-calibre at thirty paces. That's not bad shooting.

Jason Moran knew that, had I had been carrying a handgun, I would have taken his left or right eye out at a distance of five metres and he acted nervous throughout the whole rather odd and strange meeting. He put his hand out and shook mine like a limp-wrested, sweaty-handed poofter; he was shitting himself at the thought of me being armed up.

Was he armed or not? We'll never know but I know he regularly carried a 9mm during the war so I suspect he was.

The only reason he didn't pull his gun out on me and shoot me then and there on the spot, was the simple fear that the Chopper Read he knew and feared was armed up – which in the old days I always was – seven days a week, twenty-four hours a day, awake and asleep.

I was always within reach of a firearm. To be honest, had I been carrying a handgun, I think I would have put one in each kneecap, as I knew he wouldn't have given me up and it wouldn't have hurt my reputation one little bit. The only problem was I'd then have to again carry a gun at all times. I would have been back in a war that was not of my making just for a few moments' fun.

As a married man with a little baby boy to bring up, it wouldn't be worth the bother because if you carry a gun you will end up using it. At least I've found that to be the truth in my personal case. So I'm glad I was unarmed on the day.

As for Jason. I've said it before and I repeat it: he was a lowlife, weak-gutted, woman basher, rapist, drug dealer and a two-bob standover man who hung on Alphonse Gangitano's shirt-tails like a girl.

He lived in fear of Big Al; fear and admiration, but more fear than admiration.

Carl Williams did me a great personal favour when he killed the Morans, as they were the last men in Melbourne who would have been keen to pull the trigger on me – from behind, never face to face. But from behind, I knew they both had plans for me. It was only a matter of time. So 'Thank you, Carl,' I owe you a beer when you get out. It will probably cost about $1500 a pot because it will be around 2042. That's inflation for you. It's criminal.

The Shifty Deal
The Australian courts don't hold no grudge,
A nod's as good as a wink,
To a blind judge,
No need for cash, the brief's been paid,
All praise the name of Legal Aid,
The Crown is hoping for an early night,
No need to struggle,
No need to fight,
'Look, boys, I'll drop this,
'You plead to that.'
And all home in time,
To feed the cat,
No cash needed here,
Nor money down,
Forget the Yanks,
This is Melbourne town,
'I'll do this for you,
'You do that for me,
'We can sort this out,
'Just wait and see,'
The courts, crooks and coppers all know the feel,
Of the classic Aussie shifty deal.

WOMEN AND THE BATTLE OF THE SEXES

On Margaret (his second wife and lifetime love)…

'I am the perfect husband. After all, I have no ears.'

'Once she was questioned by the homicide squad over me for five hours – and stuck rock solid. She was questioned by the internal security unit three times running for hours at a time over me – and remained rock solid. She had withstood death threats too many times to count, over me. She sat though my murder trial. She has never failed me, let me down or betrayed me. She's got more heart, guts and dash than any man I've known.'

'Like all Maltese women, she has a terrible temper. The first reaction of the Maltese female when angered is to head straight into the kitchen to the knife drawer.'

'Margaret has stuck with me when I have done stupid things. She has stuck when people wanted to kill me. She stuck when I was inside. There is no one as loyal as little Margaret. If most of the two-bit crims had her dash, guts and courage, they would never tell tales out of school in police stations. She has more guts than most gunmen, more loyalty than a blood relative.'

'Anyone who knows me well knows I have the words I LOVE ITA BUTTROSE tattooed on my bum. The explanation is simple enough. All the boys in the H Division loved Ita because the only magazines we were allowed there during the early and mid-1970s were the *Readers Digest* and *Women's Weekly*.'

'The drag queen was the roughest-looking piece of work God ever shovelled guts into – a body like Maggie Tabberer and a head like Henry Bolte, topped off with a big pair of silicone tits… I stepped in and smashed the "her" over the head with a mop bucket and bit its ear off.'

'There are women banging on the gates trying to get in to visit me, others ringing the prison crying over the phone pleading to talk to me, and others writing me pornographic love letters. But when I am on the outside, things change. If I was standing in a room full of nymphomaniacs, I could swing a cat and not hit a soul.'

'A pair of long legs can walk through doors otherwise closed. A set of big tits and a pair of big eyes and an even bigger smile can float through the valley of the shadow of death like a butterfly.'

'The chick could talk the leg off an elephant and probably deep throat one as well, from the look of her. She had a mouth wider than Mick Jagger's. As a married man, I am no longer meant to notice these things, but as an author I am allowed to. It's called literary licence, and it's a lot easier to get than a gun licence. So you can all get stuffed.'

'Tracy was a top-looking babe when she had her looks and health, all legs and tits – and false teeth, which is not always a disadvantage in her line of work.'

'Falling in lust with them [prostitutes] was fine but falling in love was foolish. And should you be unlucky enough to fall in love with a cracker, then stab yourself in the back because if you don't then little Miss Tragic Magic will do it for you... It is hard to trust a girl who loves everyone and kisses each man's heart with a different lie on her lips. My problem is that in my youth I had the misfortune to fall under the spell of several ladies of the night and found myself betrayed.'

'Don't ever go shopping with your wife. I needed some new underpants. I'm now tipping the scales at a dainty eighteen stone. I waited outside the store trying to act debonair and the wife selected several pairs of extra-extra-large jockey-type underpants.

'The sales girl and her various sales-lady friends gathered as well as lady shoppers and held the offending garments up for inspection. Other ladies came over and inspected the underwear then the wife called me over. I had to walk through a small army of smiling girls, mothers, shoppers and sales ladies while the jumbo man-size lingerie was held up against my embarrassed person for further inspection. Ladies, girls, onlookers came from everywhere. Chopper Read was buying underpants. This was a must-see moment... "I just want a couple of sets of underpants," I said. "Big ones."

I was so embarrassed I would have bought anything to get out of there.

'I turned and walked out, waiting in the street outside. Then the wife followed along having purchased two pairs of jumbo jockey shorts that could have doubled as circus tents. "Don't take me shopping with you again," I said. "In future just get me big underpants, socks and T-shirts."

'I could not believe what she had just put me through. And I thought prison was bad.'

'Female lawyers can have a great bedside manner but are prone to losing cases. Never allow the charms of a lady lawyer to sway you from common sense.'

'Let's just say I knew of one lady lawyer who wore stockings and a suspender belt, stiletto high heels and the works under her black dress and robe and would allow a certain client to run his hand up her leg in the Supreme Court interview room... When a guy is locked up in prison the mind can play tricks.

'When a lady lawyer pops into the prison on a Sunday wearing runners and a baggy tracksuit and the poor prisoner is called up to the professional visit area to see his lawyer and the tracksuit pants come down and she invites the client to hump the arse off her it tends to soften the word "guilty".'

'I know a lady lawyer who was banned from jail for a few days after a misunderstanding. She was talking to her client when her blouse appeared to open all by itself. Her client became flushed and appeared quite overcome. He got life for murder but he paid her bill without complaint.'

'I've had lady lawyers and gentlemen lawyers and the best of them all was Bernie 'The Attorney' Balmer and for the record I would like to say that not once was he overcome with the impulse to show me his tits. Thank goodness.'

'Why is it that, when I am in jail and locked up like a rat in a trap, and totally unable to take advantage of any romantic situation offered to me, I manage to pull more pussy than a Chinese restaurant? Yet, when I am free and at large, girls of loose morals bite holes in screen doors trying to get away from me.'

'Of the several hundred love letters I have got in jail, I have developed a good filing system. You may remember that while in jail I have to go without a private secretary. The letters from old, ugly or fat chicks go in the bin. Cruel, you may think. Well, put it this way, if you are silly enough to write a love letter with a photo included to a self-confessed arsehole, then you better make sure you are good looking, or it's straight into the old round filing cabinet.

'I have replied to some letters, and write to a small fistful of outrageously good-looking young ladies. Just because I've got no ears doesn't mean I've got no taste.'

'In jail I would get letters from ladies that all started the same way. "This is the first time I've written to someone like you blah, blah, blah." After a bit a chit-chat they would get to the point. They would raise how I used to bash rapists in jail. Then they would say how they were molested when they were young and nothing was done about it and they would love me to visit their uncle, teacher or father – whoever did it to them – and even the score. There are a lot of bad things that have happened in the suburbs of Australia that has been hidden for years. Maybe I should have visited some of them late at night just to talk about old times.'

'If you want to know about a bloke then talk to the chick who's got him by the dick.'

'Sawn-off shotguns, chainsaws, tiger snakes and wives. If you don't take a firm grip they can jump back and bite you.'

'The point is that my feelings towards women are the same as my feelings towards men. I've met some fantastic ones and I've found some diamonds in my life, but in general they are a steaming great shower of shit that I wouldn't piss on. As a rule, if the female of the species did not provide a sexual advantage, the male of the species wouldn't even engage the buggers in conversation. Call me old-fashioned.'

'I've never killed a female, and I never could. Don't ask me why, but to me it just didn't seem right. I'm a bit of a fuddy duddy in that area.

The Greyhound Question

In the games played between men and women,
The greyhound has its place,
The two have a lot in common,
Pet them right and they'll both lick your face,
Would you swap your lady for a greyhound?
Would you ask for two or maybe three?
Speaking for myself, two's OK by me,
Three greyhounds for your sister?
And your mother? Maybe four?
And if you really love your wife,
You're allowed to ask for more,
It's a social question that presents us with a puzzle:
One wears lipstick; the other wears a muzzle.
So remember next time you come home late,
And she's tossed your dinner on the floor,
Just tell her you'll swap her for a greyhound,
Let's face it…
She can't be worth much more.

'One lady ended up in tears after proudly showing me her brand-new boob-enlargement job. Most impressive. I advised her to go back and get her face fixed as a job lot. Ha, ha. Why are people so upset by constructive criticism?'

'My wife is going to have a baby. I told her that we will have to go to the doctor and find out what caused it, then we must stop doing it right away.'

'Walking is good exercise, and I need it. Walking the dog beats spanking the monkey any day.

'Most men my age would be happy to walk Miss Nude Australia across the paddocks with a dog or two, giving new meaning to the words "watch those puppies bounce". We had two puppies, a fine pussy and half a mongrel all out in the fresh air.'

'I have pulled all the pictures of girls from my walls. I have become sick and tired of prison staff and other inmates perving on pictures of some of my good friends who happen to be female… I have decided to get rid of them because with some of the comments made about them I would end up pulling some bastard's eye out, which would not look good when I am trying to convince the High Court that I am the male version of Mother Teresa. So I have put up pictures of the Derwent Valley in their place. It has helped calm everyone down, me included. I have never had a dream of covering the Derwent Valley with whipped cream and then licking it off.'

'It's quite amazing. Here I sit with a no-eared toothless head that even a mother wouldn't love and I've got the screws at Risdon Jail shooing the sheilas away with a stick. God's idea of a practical joke? I can't figure it out.'

'Women understand sex, but they do not understand the psychology of fear. For women the answer is simple. Understand what is happening to you and, if you don't like it, smile, play along nicely and stab the bastard in the back at the first opportunity. Ha. Ha.'

'I don't know what it is about ladies and guns, but there is a definite psychological effect when you mix the two. They get an excited gleam in their eyes and just blast away as if there is no tomorrow.'

'Men are cunning rats. They pretend to be civilised and domesticated, but underneath that they are slobs. Always have been and always will be. Mind you, most women suspect the truth. And that is that men are like lino tiles... lay them the right way once and you can walk over them forever.'

'Women who fall in love with men in jail are nearly always disappointed. The first thing you learn on the inside is to say what people want to hear and make promises you have no intention of keeping. You tell the Parole Board you have reformed, the guard you have no idea who bashed the dickhead in the next cell and your new girlfriend you will always be faithful.

'It's like a dog on a chain. You put the dog on the chain for the night then let him off the chain in the morning and he runs around and around the back yard like a raving nutter.

'You lock a man in a cage for a year or two or longer, then let him out, and you're going to be a sad girl if you think he's going to come home and sit in front of the telly with a tinny, 24 hours a day.'

'All my life since my teenage years I've always had and kept the friendship of females, and I am by no means a romantic or a playboy.

'I think the answer is that I always treated ladies like I treated men: with sarcastic disregard, yet blind loyalty when the shit hit the fan. I treat them as mates. Most of the female friends I've had and still have to this day have never been romantically involved with me.

'I've put holes in my manners with a fair few of them but, as I keep telling the buggers, what's the use of having mates with tits if you cannot get the buggers to knock the top off it now and again, for Christ's sake?'

Written when single (Sorry, Margaret)

'As far as females are concerned I am totally schizophrenic. It is like being in a giant lolly shop. There I am happily munching away on a Pollywaffle then someone hands me a Snickers funsize. "Oh goodie," I say. I am halfway through that when someone tosses me a Mars Bar and I am into that. And the next thing you know I am into the liquorice allsorts. Then come the Tim Tams, when all of a sudden I spy the deluxe selection of fruit-flavoured soft-centred assortments. Whacko! I am just about to make a pig of myself when along comes a sales lady with – yes, you guessed it – an all-day sucker.

'It's like heaven and hell and I am lost in my own indulgence. When I am running around on the outside, even though my heart may belong to one lady, I can't help sampling whatever's on offer. I also realise that the axe can fall on me at any moment and the "eat, drink and be merry – for tomorrow I die" mentality takes hold.'

'I find this, in its way, quite sad. Some of my best mates are women. Sure, I may have plonked a few of them along the way, but they are essentially good mates. They have remained rock solid when a few of the so-called tough guys of the underworld have caved in as soon as the cops have said "boo".'

'After a lifetime of study, I have come up with what I believe to be a rock-solid doctrine on the vexing topic of female of the species, and it would be selfish of me not to share it.

'I see all females without exception as suffering from a mental and emotional psychosis that I call "the schizophrenic condition". It isn't their fault; it's just the way it is. They tend to be insecure, afraid, puzzled, confused, worried, concerned, ill at ease and lacking self-esteem and self-confidence. Not only that, they are dizzy, scatty, flighty, totally withdrawn from reality and tend to totally distort reality. And loving, hateful, possessive, jealous, greedy, generous, dreamers and fantasy merchants living in a world of romantic imagination… they have a list of mental and emotional disorders a mile long all on the boil. Add the sex and the motherhood urge to this and you have a totally neurotic, obsessive, anxious, head banging, raving, ranting nutcase of the highest and most dangerous order.

'In other words, the classic schizophrenic condition. We are talking about human beings who undergo twelve separate mood swings every twelve hours.'

'They can get through childbirth and then whine about a stubbed toe. They seem to hate silence unless they are mad and then they decide not to talk to you for decades.

'They can't read a map, have no sense of direction but always insist on telling you when they think you are going the wrong way.

'Don't tell them they look sexy and they sulk. Tell them they've got great tits and they reckon you treat them as sex object.

'Mind you, I hope you don't think that my attitude towards females means that I hate women. I love them. They are beautiful, magical and fascinating creatures and it's just that I view both males and females as suffering from two forms of mental and emotional psychosis.

'In a sense, I see all men as killers and all women as whores. Not all men are physical killers, of course. Only a small percentage of the male population will actually kill, but all men carry a very strong killer instinct within them.

'And of course not all women are whores, but the whore instinct is within every woman. We all know in our hearts that this is true, no matter how much we may deny it. In fact, denying the unpleasant truth to ourselves is all part of the general insanity that goes to make up the human condition.'

'The imagination of every female secretly longs for the knight in shining armour to ride up on his snow-white charger and dry her tears, sweep her off her feet and gallop off into the sunset.'

'Men are putty in a woman's hands. They all want to impress, first their mothers, then their teachers and then girlfriends and wives.

'They climb mountains, sail across seas and even shoot drug dealers so that some sheila somewhere will say, "Well done." When a footballer wins the Brownlow the player thanks his blonde wife or girlfriend. For what? Did she feed him one in the goal-square? Who knows, maybe she did.

'I have secretly always believed that in the battle of the sexes the female has always had the ability to play the male like a fine violin.'

Lady Killer

I never killed a lady, and I really don't know why,
Most of the ones I've met have really
deserved to die,
I guess in the end,
In spite of my mind being bent,
I'm just a bloody old softy,
A real old-fashioned gent.

BEING AN AUTHOR

'If bastards and bad men are so hated, why do good men love to read about them?'

'Some may think the pen is mightier than the sword, but don't take either to a gun fight.'

'I have written a book and people seem to think I walk about all day in a smoking jacket stuffed full of cash and live on champagne and caviar. In fact, people think I have become a millionaire through writing. Let me tell you I made more money with a blowtorch than a ballpoint. And I didn't get too much out of the crime world either.'

'There is the elite class – killer poets like my good self who can write, fight, bite, light, smite and, when need be, say goodnight.'

'While I was inside, I got mail by the truckload. Much of it is nice but some is rather puzzling.

'I have heard from literary critics and lounge-chair intellectuals telling me that my books have no real message. Well, first of all, the only literary critic I really care about is the cash register, and when it stops ringing I will know I have hit a false note.

'As far as intellectuals are concerned, an intellectual is someone who spends all his time giving other people the answers to questions he didn't understand in the first place. They go through life dreaming up new ways to fix problems that they themselves created.

'I never went out to write a book that had a special message. If you played it backwards on your record player, it wouldn't tell you what really happened to Elvis.'

'I wish I could debate my literary efforts with other respected and well-known authors over a sherry and Greek dip. Instead, I am sure that if I met most of the people who have read my work I would have to ask them to stop weaving their baskets before we could discuss their views on my writing.'

'When I write the truth, I am faced with verbal bullets from my critics and real ones from my enemies. Words are like magic stardust to be thrown into the eyes of men to confuse and inform at the same time.

'The pen is mightier than the sword, but in fairness to the sword great things have been done by men and swords. But without the pen the actions of the sword would not be remembered beyond one generation.'

'She [first wife Mary-Ann] once called me away from my writing to come and see the way Poop Foot our cat was sitting. Do all great writers have to put up with this? No wonder Hemingway topped himself. At least he had a double-barrelled shotgun to do it with.'

'Fact is stranger than fiction – sometimes so strange that it is downright hard to believe – they shout and laugh at reality, or maybe truth is a bit humdrum and ordinary for them. The fiction writer can turn a bullet in the guts into an epic thriller, whereas in reality a slug in the guts is not worth more than a page.

'An act of violence, whether broken glass in the neck, or a bullet in a body, is over in the blink of an eye, and to write about it should not take more than a page or so. That is why I will never be accepted as a proper writer by other writers. I tell it how it is… bang, bang, and no bullshit, then on to the next story. I have been there, I have done it and for mine you cannot turn a ten-second stabbing into a ten-chapter epic. Not unless you are a fiction writer, that is. And I'm a fighter, not a writer. I know about verbals not verbs. Guns, not grammar.'

'If the authorities tried to stop some government-subsidised, black T-shirt-wearing, academic trendy of questionable sexuality, from writing some boring sixty-page book about the mating habits of Tibetan yaks, the civil libertarians would be protesting in the streets.

'But because the author is a Good Ol' Boy with no ears, who is popular with the public, and therefore not seen as trendy, then no one has lifted a finger.'

'Posh people love gangsters.'

'The truth is that all I ever wanted to do was write a cook

book. I was going to call it: *How to Kill Them in the Kitchen*. But Mick Gatto beat me to it. I could dedicate it to Andrew Veniamin, who got a case of terminal indigestion.'

'Pregnant women are a beautiful thing, but you could get whiplash trying to keep up with the mood swings.

'Sadly, when she should be concentrating on sleeping and getting bigger with our unborn son, she decides to become a part-time literary critic.'

'I know I have finally made it as a top-class writer after all these years. Like Mark Twain and Oscar Wilde I have been declared bankrupt. In the old days I knew ten drug dealers who could have helped me out once I showed them a little bit of blowtorch persuasion. Sometimes I regret going straight but you can't get blood from a stone-killer.'

WRITING

So my writing upsets the toffs, the politicians and the cops,
But when ya jump on the horse, ya flog her till she drops,
And I guess now I will have to call it quits,
It's hard yakka brother, and I must say it's giving me the shits,
I've written about mugs and molls and ladies of easy persuasion,
About the poets of old, and the cultural Yank invasion,
I've written about the pros and cons of every bloomin' thing,
Knocked up songs no man will ever sing,
And every word's been done with just a touch of comic malice,

And all from my little cell in the old Pink Palace.
But the time has come to turn it up, 'cos it's messing up my mind,
And as my old dad used to say, 'Stop it, son, or you'll go blind,'
So this is it, I swear to God, and of that I am quite certain,
I've written down my last verse, reached my final curtain,
It's time to toss my pen and paper in the fire.
But you and me both know that I'm a shocking liar,
And it's easy to see if you look at me,
And all the times I've been busted,
That when I say I'll walk away…
You know I can't be trusted.

'I didn't get these scars in a fight over the sushi tray at a crime writers' conference, and the claw-hammer hole in my head didn't come from a dispute with the scone lady over the strawberry jam.'

'I always feel uncomfortable when anyone asks me for my autograph. I'm not a rock star; I'm a crook who wrote a book, and the psychology of wanting an autograph from me is wanting it for its novelty freak value.'

MANNERS AND DINING

'I've dug a few graves in my time. But I have never made a man dig his own. There's no need to go that far – it would be plain bad manners.'

'I swallowed my own top teeth myself years ago. They bloody nearly killed me going down and it was an uncomfortable experience getting them out the other end.

'So the message to all you kiddies is, brush after meals so that you don't end up with false teeth. Otherwise it can hurt both ends.'

'I am without a shadow of a doubt the fastest eater in captivity, bar maybe the odd polar bear in a zoo somewhere.

'I can shovel down steak, eggs, sausages, mushrooms and mixed veggies and sweets in under three minutes with total propriety. I have perfect manners. I eat like Prince Charles would if he was on Angel Dust.'

'I love all types of food, although at times I'm a little wary of your Chinese tucker. You would be, too, if you knew which crims used to be shipped off to a certain dim sim factory where they went on the missing list. It happened so often it became the norm, if you know what I mean.

'Now I have been close to many members of the criminal fraternity, but not close enough to eat them with soy sauce and fried rice.

'I know life can be sweet and sour but that is ridiculous.'

On Japanese food. 'They give you raw fish, no chips, no knife and fork and charge you thirty bucks for the privilege. And they call me a criminal.'

'We made Reggie eat his own fox terrier. But it wasn't all bad. We had garlic salt, cooking oil, salt and pepper, plus American mustard. After all, we weren't savages.'

'Willie Thompson sold lollipops when he was shot dead, Michael Marshall did a roaring trade in hot dogs when he was popped off, Mark Moran made pies and sausage rolls when he was a pastry chef and Normie Lee had a dim sim factory before police shot him dead – proving once and for all that junk food is a killer. Bring on meat and three veg. Yummy.'

'On my daily walks to the prison hospital from the remand yard to get my vitamin tablet, I found, much to my delight, seven big, fat snails, bloody big buggers. Anyone who has been to jail knows that all prisoners become first-class scroungers and learn that anything they can find to use they will grab with both hands.

'Now the sight of seven snails was too great a temptation to me. I scooped the blighters up and asked one of the screws to boil up some water for me. I placed the snails in the water and let them soak for about ten minutes. I then got some more boiling water and gave them another ten minutes. That seemed to slow them down, in a manner of speaking. They were easy then to pop out of their shells.

'I got hold of some silver paper, some salt, pepper, garlic powder and a spoonful of butter. I didn't have a French cookbook so I had to do the best I could. In prison, nouvelle cuisine is anything cooked by a first-year apprentice cook. I got the recently deceased snails, minus their shells, and wrapped them in the silver paper, with the salt, pepper, butter and garlic powder. I placed the lot on the grill under the big toaster in the remand yard dining room. I felt I was getting the hang of the French cooking. In fact, with my experience with meat cleavers I thought that when I got out of jail I would go into the culinary business.

'I was confident, perhaps too confident, about my cooking skills. The little buggers finally had their revenge. I had plenty of time to think about my mistakes as I was sitting on the toilet. I know about severe stomach pains, having been stabbed in the guts once or twice, and, let me tell you, the snails were tougher than a steak-knife attack.

'I was shivering and shaking and thought I was at death's door. I have suffered bad cases of Bombay Bottom, at the hands of Mad Dog's curried veggies in Pentridge and Slim Minogue's chilli powder delights, but that pales into nothing compared with the revenge of the killer snails.

'It was then I learned a very important lesson about cooking the more exotic dishes. If one insists on eating garlic snails, one should always know that the snails themselves have not gobbled a gutful of snail bait. The little green pellets turned out to be snail poison and the buggers I had been eating were the gung-ho survivors of more chemicals than Chernobyl.'

'As a cook. my mum would have made a great steam cleaner. Everything I ate was either steamed or boiled.'

'I knew a copper once who said his wife was a dirty, lazy bitch. He said, "I came home after a night on the squirt, had a piss in the sink and there were the dishes from breakfast still sitting there."'

'I believe that men should not be allowed to assist in the preparation of any food for health reasons.

'Now, men don't like to talk about it, but they all have one thing in common when it comes to the kitchen: they all end up pissing in the sink. There is not a man living who has not at one time or another pissed in the sink.'

'He [Brian Murphy – legendary hard-nosed detective] was raised a strict Catholic and it is said he is more frightened of an angry priest than a hundred angry crims. He only has to see a priest or a nun half a mile away and he takes his bloody hat off.'

The Skull

Murphy was the master of the bullshit and the baffle,
He'd be in anything from a gunfight to a raffle,
From a gun butt to a head butt, he dropped a hundred men,
He's fight them 'til they couldn't stand,
Then he'd do it all again,
He loved to go a round or two,
This tough old Melbourne jack,
He lost his gold clubs down the docks,
But by God he got them back,

Love him or hate him, the could never call him dull,
A bloody Melbourne legend,
Was the cop they called 'The Skull'.

PRISON

'Just because a man is sent to prison does not end his interests in the crime world. Certain drug king pins and upmarket drug dealers still operate and control their business from behind bluestone walls. A host of bank robberies are planned, put together and ordered from behind bars and carried outside by friends or helpers.

'The amount of crime that is carried out on the orders of men serving sentences is amazing. The amount of crime controlled from behind prison walls would stagger most people.'

'I love a good criminal war or battle situation and I am only ever consulted on matters of violence and death.'

'I am a bit lucky that the blows to the head I have received over the years have done something to my timing. I can be in jail for years and years and the time doesn't seem to mean much. It is a bit worrying, but it may have done me a favour.'

'The Australian penal system is a sick, corrupt, drug-infested cesspit of mental illness, perversion and despair where violence is part of daily routine.'

'But hard rules apply behind the bluestone walls. They may

be sick and sorry rules, but they are rules of the wild. The strong rule and the weak cry. The criminal world, both inside and outside the jail, is ruled through strength. It is not a democracy.'

'The modern prison is a marshmallow compared with good old H. It was the last place from the old hard school and in my heart I preferred the old days to the system that we have now. A good flogging can concentrate the mind.

'I did more than 10 years in "H", the so-called blood house of the system. It wasn't just my home, I owned the place. I owned it, I controlled it, I ran it. By ruling that division we ran the jail. We were the most feared gang in the most feared division of the most feared jail in Australia and I was the commanding general.'

'We had a war in jail because I was alleged to have eaten too many sausages, a foul piece of slander indeed – although I must say they were yummy.'

'The Overcoat Gang War, which went five years inside Pentridge, was probably the bloodiest crime war in Victoria. But because it was waged inside jail very little was ever heard about it on the outside. G Division … was the area kept in jail for the mentally unwell. I had obviously been put there by mistake, ha ha. I was actually sent there after I mislaid my ears. Obviously, those in power thought this was not the act of a well unit.'

'I am confident that I hold the bashing record inside Pentridge and it will never be beaten because the jail is now structured differently.

'I would say the Overcoat War saw well over a hundred separate attacks over five years before some of us went to Jika and couldn't get each other as often.

'The war ended in 1980 because they sent some of us to Jika Jika when it first opened. There were a few half-hearted attempts to keep it going but we just couldn't get at each other any more.

'Prisoner violence was considered the pastime of the 1970s. Back then some of the screws and the governors encouraged it. They thought it was akin to a bloody good football match. It kept the prison population busy and gave them something to think about.

'The jail governors today are a little limp-wristed when it comes to matters of violence. Since the 1980s, drugs and violence have ruled the jail, but the class of men and the class of violence is very petty. Savage and evil, yes, but very petty.

'In the 1970s, the jail was ruled by home brew and iron bars. The violence raged from one end of the place to the other. The press got told very little about it. The younger crims today simply find it hard to believe the stories of blood and guts that went on inside and outside jail.

'These days the so-called top crims are so full of junk they couldn't change their underwear. Outside it is the same. The gang bosses and the drug lords get rid of their enemies by ringing the police. They demand police protection if their own lives are threatened. The guts and courage have gone. The criminal scene is just a sea of vomit. But back in the days of the Overcoat War there was plenty of full-on guts and courage on both sides.

'Our side was outnumbered but we had some great tactical advantages. We had a spy network right through the prison and we had the moral support and the blind-eye encouragement of a handful of the most right-wing, broken-nosed, cauliflower-eared, hired-by-the-pound, knuckles scraping on the ground, leg-breaking screws any jail has ever seen. We also had one big bonus, the blessing of Jimmy Quinn, the Pentridge Governor of Security.

'When the blood starts flying, I'll do business with the Devil himself. Victory at all costs is the only thing. You can discuss the moral ethics as we bury the enemy. That's how I got away with it all for five years: I had a friend in high places.

'Governor Quinn died in the early 1980s. He was a grand old fellow, a man who would have a drink on any occasion. He loved to bet, a fight, and blood and guts – and he thought the world of me and I of him. In the 1970s, Jimmy Quinn once had his nose broken in a punch-on with a Painter and Docker who was my enemy in B Division. So, when the Overcoat War broke out, Jimmy Quinn took my side. My enemy already had a few high-ranking prison staff on side, but I had all the old-time blood-and-guts brigade. After all, it was a prison war between inmates, but we were fighting on the screws' playing field, so some friends at court were needed on both sides. I think my enemy went through the whole war wishing he hadn't broken the governor's nose.

'Through Governor Quinn I could get into other prisoners' cells at night, get into other yards and get prisoners transferred from one division to another, have my own men moved. The pull I had was quite unbelievable. Quinn used to send two security screws down to H Division early in the morning to handcuff me and bring me up to the security office and into his office. I'd be uncuffed there and the governor would sit down with me, his office door closed, and we'd drink coffee and eat Choc Royal bikkies and watch slides of his latest overseas holidays. Now and again, we would break out a small bottle of whisky or a can or two of beer. At the height of the Overcoat War, he once had me brought to his office and over a can of beer he explained to me that, for every dozen or so bashing and attacks that Overcoat Gang did, only one would get mentioned on any report, and none, if any, on my personal records. It was getting a bit tropical and I had to ease it up for a while. The A Division bomb had just gone off and Quinn was under pressure. He then said that every twelve or so bashings one would get a mention.

When I cut my ears off, Governor Quinn came to hospital to visit me. When I got stabbed he also came in to see me. He was a good mate with my dad. He was not a corrupt man. He was just an old-style blood-and-guts boy, and a good war in jail gave us all something to do. He was a grand old fellow, and his death was a great sadness to me personally.'

'One of Jimmy Loughnan's favourite party tricks in H Division during the war was to get hold of chaps we felt had been 'putting holes in their manners'. [Loughnan was Read's right-hand man until he turned on him, stabbing him in jail. Loughnan later died in a jail fire.] We would grab the offending party and give him a touch-up – otherwise known as a sound beating. Then we would stand him up. I'd put a butcher's knife to his neck and Jimmy would put a razor blade in his mouth and he would be told to chew on it.

'There would be a little protest at first, but it was a case of chew or die – and a mouth full of blood was better than a neck full of cold steel. So chew, it would be. If you've never seen a man chew a razor blade, you have never seen blood flow. There would be choking and coughing and blood – sometimes vomiting. It was a lesson once learned, never forgotten. It must have been pain beyond description. But H Division in the 1970s was a blood-soaked mental hospital of violence and more violence – and only the truly ultra-violent could rule it. The list of weapons made and used in Pentridge goes on and on, and we used them all. There are iron bars, claw hammers, garden spades, homemade tomahawks, ice picks, screwdrivers sharpened to pinpoint, nun-chukkas, meat cleaver and butcher knives from the kitchen.

'My favourite was a razor blade welded into the end of a toothbrush with a cigarette lighter, or a blade with sticky-tape wrapped around one end. When it is held between the thumb and the forefinger with a flash of the wrist you can open a man's face up like a ripe watermelon.'

'One trick we used that I can now admit was the soap scam. A dirty trick but it was a jail gang war, so all was fair...

'I got a dozen bars of soap, soaked them in a plastic bucket of hot water for 15 minutes, the pulled them out and a slid a razor blade down the side of each bar. Then I left them out in the sun to harden.

'I was in H Division number-one billet at the time. My job was serving out the meals, cleaning the cells, the wing, the labour yard and the shower yard – meaning I had total run of the division. I removed all soap from the shower yards, and put six blocks of my trick soap in each shower yard.

'Needless to say, without going into the bloody details, it worked a treat. My enemies were not only frightened to eat their food – for fear of rat poison or human shit in the stew – they couldn't even use soap in the showers without fear. I was mentally destroying their will. I would leave dobs of jam under their beds to attract ants. I'd piss in their cordial bottles. Along with the bloody violence and physical beatings, these added touches reduced my enemies to tears – and total surrender.'

'Why did I have my ears chopped off? ... I told them, "I will be leaving H Division, tomorrow." They said, "No, you won't," and I said I would. So I went back and got Kevin to cut my bloody ears off. You reckon I didn't leave H Division straight away? The classo board nearly came down and carried me out themselves.

'The first time it happened it was big news, then everyone started doing it, nothing to do with me. Then all the nutcases in here thought there was something to be gained out of this. I was the president of the Van Gogh club until Garry David cut his penis off. I wrote to him, "You can take over." When the dicky birds start hitting the pavement I thought it was time to resign.

'Enduring a bit of pain is one thing, but that's a bit much.'

'The man who cut them [ears] off was Kevin James Taylor, the chap doing life for shooting Pat Shannon. If a man tries to cut off his own ears, he will make a pig's breakfast of the job, so I asked Kevin to do it for me. I went into the number-one shower yard of H Division, sat down, folded my arms and sat as still as I could.

'Kevin had the razor blade. I said, "OK, do it." He started to do it really gently and slow, but that was very painful. I said, "Come on, you bloody fairy, rip into it," and so he did.

'I remember the sound, it was like running your fingernails down a blackboard at school, only it was going through my head, then I felt the warm blood bubbling in my ears. Then he did the second one. I thought Van Gogh had done it, so it couldn't be life threatening. I decided to have a cold shower and all the bleeding would stop. But it just wouldn't slow down at all.

'The blood flowed and flowed after the ears came off, the rest of the guys freaked out. They thought I'd gone crazy. Kevin knocked on the yard door and the screws let me out. We all said I'd cut my ears off because we didn't want to get Kevin in trouble. He's out now so it doesn't matter.

'The doctors didn't believe me, but, when I looked down on the ground at my fallen ears, I was sure I could see them doing an Irish jig. Maybe I was seeing things or maybe it was the nerves in the ears making them twitch.'

'Kill me or cop it sweet, that's the way I saw it. In or out of prison, no one could take more pain than me, no one could dish out more pain than me. I wasn't about to stand in the shadow of any man who went before me.'

'I'm already punch drunk in charge of limited intelligence as it is.'

'Ahh, Chopper, you old trendsetter. But, as I said to the boys, if you really want to look like the Chopper, get them bloody ears off. The mention of a razor blade slicing through the ears soon separates the men from the boys.'

'There is no evidence of psychiatric disorder in Mr Read. He clearly has a most unusual personality, but then, that would be expected of someone who is not uncomfortable about being regarded as a professional criminal.'

From a psychiatric report on Mark Brandon Read

'Some prisoners like to waffle on about the dark and lonely solitude of their damp and lonely cell and how they never forgot the sound of the cell door slamming for the first time.

What a load of crap. One cell is the same as any other. When you have heard one cell door slam, you have heard them all. Jail life can be summed up in two words: petty and boring.'

'After the years that I have done inside, I would write a thousand pages on jail life. But men who have done it, lived it, bled it, cried and nearly died in it couldn't be bothered.

'I'll leave that all to one-month wonders, who can write a gripping thriller based on their blood-chilling adventures in Her Majesty's Motel.'

'If you are a police informer or an offender against small children, you can buy yourself all the friends and supporters you want with a gram of heroin. Not like the old days when a child molester could look forward to having a mop inserted in his bottom and then be flogged to within an inch of his pathetic life.'

'Police informers, crown witnesses, child killers and molesters openly running about the jails of the nation without a care in the world, and some of them swaggering about like gangsters… it's enough to make you sick.'

FRIENDS AND ENEMIES

'I had a deep sense of friendship, but over the years the more knives that got stuck in my back and the more times I was betrayed, that sense of friendship becomes less and less.'

'To be stabbed by the same bloke that I tried to get out of jail is a terrible lesson, a good lesson, but a hard way to learn.'

'In my enemies' rush to condemn me, to destroy me with venom and outrage, they have, in fact, almost given me a legal licence to kill – in self-defence, of course. The plea of self-defence is rarely used in court and believed even less. In my case, it is a simple case of some poor bastard trying to kill Chopper Read again (yawn) as these plots against me are considered commonplace.

'If I have so many enemies, who can I trust? As far as trust is concerned, the old saying that there are no friends in business applies a hundred-fold in the criminal world. In the name of self-interest and survival, most men will betray a friend to save their own skins, or further their own ends. There are a few men who are exceptions to this rule, even fewer in the criminal world.

'Chopper's golden rule is that, when the shit hits the fan, keep an eye on the people closest to you. The graveyards are full of blokes who got put there by their friends.'

'Friendship is a funny thing. When the good times roll, everyone wants to rock and roll with you and when the shit hits the fan you're on your own.'

'The enemy of my enemy is my friend.'

'Tears mean nothing when they are insincere. Even real tears can conceal a murderer.'

'And I am a man with a long, long memory. Shallow people and false pretenders don't have long memories. They will forget, but I won't. I don't have to shoot people to punish them. There are more ways to kill a cat than by wringing its neck. The cats in question used up their nine lives when they betrayed my trust and friendship.'

'Any fool could see that Alphonse was running red-hot and couldn't be allowed to keep going. But then again, I'm no fool.'

'Alphonse was a fool for trusting such a weak-gutted arse-wipe as Jason Moran. Jason was at best a woman basher and a two-bob bullyboy. He never fought anyone who could fight and never made a move against anyone who had real dash or guts.'

'Nothing that happens these days seems the same as it once was, and while I live in the present I constantly miss the dead friends of old. All my life people have been coming into my life leaving their mark on my mind, heart and soul, and then dying on me or vanishing into the mists of time. It makes me sad and sentimental.'

SID COLLINS

Read was jailed for shooting Collins in Tasmania. The former president of an outlaw motorcycle gang, Collins was reported missing in NSW in September 2001 and his body has never been found.

'No, 1992 certainly wasn't Sid's year. He got shot and married.'

(1994) 'According to rumour, Sid is now involved in an area of work that, to put it politely, I do not agree with. All in all, his life is not filled with joy.'

'I knew that Sid had an appointment with a bullet — it was just a matter of when. Why did I know this? Because Sid had his own enemies.

'Pumping a slug into someone's leg or guts is no big deal in Melbourne or Sydney. If Sid needed a shot in the guts to teach him to pull up his socks, it was none of my concern.

'I cannot write that I did in fact shoot the tip rat – as that would mean a charge of perjury being laid against me – as I swore in the Tasmanian Supreme Court that I didn't shoot Collins.'

MURDERER ALEX TSAKMAKIS

'A mass killer, a coward, an egomaniac... I leaned over his shoulder, snatched the pair of scissors and stabbed him in the neck. I later dipped my fingers in his blood and wrote on his cell door, "Sorry about that, Alex."

'But Alex did teach me to play chess – and for that I thank him.'

BARRY ROBERT QUINN

A guru-like criminal who inspired killings without actually committing them. 'His was cowardly violence of a mindless nature directed against the weak without courage, style or flair.'

TREVOR PETTINGILL, ACCUSED POLICE KILLER

'He is and will always remain a two-bob nothing little punk in a posh suit his mummy bought him. In spite of his acquittal along with others in the Walsh Street shootings, he will remain involved in crime. He has lived off the reputation of his elder brothers for years.'

PETER GIBB

Escaped with Archie Butterly from the Melbourne Remand Centre on 7 March 1993 with the help of Gibb's lover, prison officer Heather Parker. Gibb was recaptured and Butterly was shot dead.

'I've known Peter Gibb for twenty years. He is an old hood who grew up in Prahran. The first time he came to my attention was at a dance in Prahran, when a handgun dropped out of his pants and hit the floor. All eyes turned to see a somewhat embarrassed and sheepish Peter bend down to pick up the offending firearm and try to tip-toe out without drawing attention to himself.

'He was always good at pulling the girls and little Miss Parker, if my memory serves me correctly, would be the third female prison officer to fall for Peter's glib tongue.

'They all gave Peter their hearts, as well as their panties.

'He must have a good line of conversation because I have seen Peter in the showers, and, believe me, he hasn't got a big line in anything else. Ha ha.'

JOHN WILLIAM PALMER, ARMED ROBBER

'The key to Palmer was that he couldn't fight – which made him even more dangerous with a gun in his hand.'

GREGORY DAVID ROBERTS,
ALSO KNOWN AS 'DOC' SMITH

Robber, adventurer and drug addict who spent years in jail with Read. He escaped, travelled the world before being recaptured and sent back to Pentridge. On his return, Read wrote, 'He had tears in his eyes. It was good to see him. He is an ultra-smart, good-natured, almost loving man and it is very hard not to like him. What can I say? His story and adventures would fill volumes.'

Read was right. Roberts' massive book *Shantaram* is a worldwide bestseller and has been sold to Hollywood. Hollywood star Johnny Depp is preparing to play the role of Roberts.

RUSSELL 'MAD DOG' COX, ARMED ROBBER
AND ESCAPE ARTIST

'He was told that I was out to kill him and I was told that he was going to kill me. We both felt that our first meeting would be in the streets with guns blazing… Now that we are friends, the only thing we fight about is when he puts too much garlic in our lunchtime curry.

'He even won $15,000 on Tattslotto while on the run. Jesus Christ, I've shot people for less money than that.'

Russell

There was a wild Australian boy,
Russell was his name,
He was born in Sydney town,
Five miles from Balmain,
Born to be an outlaw,
He loved robbing banks,
He loved to rob the money,
And tell the tellers, 'thanks',
The coppers missed him a hundred times,
He left them in a mess,
With Russell running down the street,
Wearing a lady's dress.

JAMES EDWARD 'JOCKEY' SMITH, SHOT DEAD BY POLICE IN DECEMBER 1992

'He had a reputation as a tightwad… a man who could have a hundred grand under the bed and go out and pinch a rubbish bin rather than pay cash for it.'

JIMMY LOUGHNAN, READ'S BEST FRIEND IN JAIL

Read attempted to take a County Court judge hostage in a doomed plan to force authorities to release Loughnan. Eventually, Loughnan repaid Read's misguided loyalty by stabbing him in a sneak attack inside Pentridge. Jimmy died in a prison fire in 1987.

When Read recovered from his stab wounds, he finally ran into Loughnan inside Pentridge.

'He couldn't fight but he wasn't a coward, so he stood his ground and braced himself for the expected bashing. I walked up and kissed him on the cheek and said, "Don't worry, Jimmy, I'm not going to hurt you. Your own life will destroy you." He said, "Yeah, I know it will."

'As I walked away he called out to me, "It wasn't personal, Chopper."

'I kept walking and didn't turn back. I had tears in my eyes… I wasn't angry and I didn't hate him; he just broke my heart.'

NICK APOSTOLIDIS

'I burned Nick the Greek's house down. Big deal. If you met him, you'd want to burn it down too.'

ON HIS FRIEND, HITMAN 'DAVE THE JEW'

'Poor Dave was an intelligent teenager who ended up being probably the best secret hitman in Australia – and a man who liked to "experiment" on his victims in a way that made even me shiver. He was convinced he was the reincarnation of the American Jewish gangster Bugsy Siegel. Now in times of high unemployment this is not a good thing to put on one's CV. Imagine it. Name: Bugsy Siegel. Occupation: 1930s US Gangster. References: Al Capone, Eliot Ness and Meyer Lansky.

'Poor Dave, I love him. I often think back and see in my mind's eye myself and the Jew sitting beside Squizzy Taylor's grave (born 29 June 1888; died 26 October 1927) talking of the future. The trouble was that we were so hell bent on trying to control our destinies that we both forgot we had no control over our fate.

'One of the strangest things about Dave, as the son of strict Jewish parents, was his constant reading of Adolf Hitler's *Mein Kampf.* I asked him one day why he read such a book and he looked at me and replied quietly, "Know thy enemy."

'Dave has always been a deep thinker. He said, "Forgiveness and funerals go hand in hand and the only time to forgive an enemy is after you have seen him die.

'"If we lose this war I'll start another one in my wife's name."

'Dave shot him in both legs with a sawn-off .22. We dug the slugs out with a potato knife. Johnny then went to hospital. No slugs, no police.'

The Jew

He wants no glory, he wants no fame,
Very few men have heard his name.
But as a hunter, he's the best I know
Non-stop dash, non-stop go,
He sets to work, without a care,
The smell of burning flesh in the air,
He loves to hunt the big deal prankster,
The nightclub flashy gangster,
He plants them in the ground,
Never to be seen,
Safe and sound,
And before they die, they sometimes ask,

Please tell me who are you,
And with a toothless grin, he looks down and says,
Just call me Dave the Jew.

'When I came back from Tasmania I knew that I had wasted most of my life. Back with Margaret I was determined to have one last go at not going back to crime. But old friends – blood loyal soldiers – wanted to claim me back. I had to cut them loose. If I had taken up with them again, we would have joined the war. We would now all be dead or in jail. They will never know that I saved their lives by turning my back on them.'

DRUG DEALERS

'Now, if they had a "shoot a drug-dealer in the eye competition", I am sure I would win the gold.'

'One drug dealer I killed – as a matter of fact, he died of shock halfway through a kneecapping – had bragged of overdosing about fifty prostitutes and junkies over a ten-year period in the western suburbs. How could his death be classed as murder?'

'I'm no murderer… I'm a garbage-disposal expert.'

'Shoot a terrorist and they give you the keys to the city. Shoot a drug dealer who is killing our kids for money and you get eight years. At least the terrorist believes in what he is doing.'

'I find the selling of drugs to be a girlish, limp-wristed way to earn one's living. It is the wimp's way to gain wealth and power. Why should I steal or deal drugs when I can simply rob the drug seller?'

'There are two main reasons why I target drug dealers. First, they are the ones with the big money. One is hardly going to make a big profit from kidnapping and torturing men who pinch washing machines for a living, so it's simply a matter of logical economics.'

'I don't know why Sydney crooks don't stick to what they know best, pimping for whores and selling drugs to kids. Every time you see a Sydney crook on television, he is either lying in the street after being killed by an imported Melbourne hitman, or giving Crown evidence against some poor bastard.'

'I have been described as a monster, but what sort of monster am I supposed to be?

'I am a monster who has never hurt a woman, a child or an old person. The general public screams for the blood of child killers and child sex offenders, but, when Chopper Read bashes or stabs one of these vermin, the courts turn on me and call me a danger to the public.

'The general public screams for the blood of drug dealers, but, when I put a blowtorch to the feet of a few drug peddlers, and shoot a few more, the courts declare me the dangerous one.

'I am a monster who has not turned his hand to an innocent

member of the general public, except for the time I attacked Judge Martin, and even then we ended up writing to each other. He forgave me for what I did and I still feel bad about it.

'The courts say that the people I have hurt are members of the public and should be protected. Hang on; I thought the public was meant to be protected from sex offenders and drug pushers. Yet, when I spill a little of their blood, suddenly this lot of vermin are promoted to general public class. Are members of the criminal underworld really members of the general public? Should they be protected? Do they deserve the same rights as the rest of the community? Or is the truth that they have chosen a path in a dog-eat-dog world, so they should cop what they get and not whinge about it?

'Justice Cox, in Tassie, said that it appeared that all my violence had been directed towards members of the criminal underworld, and then declared me a danger to the general public.

'Now, call me a social buffoon, but what is what and who is whom? A drug dealer is either an enemy of the public or a member of the public. He cannot be both. The whole argument is nonsensical to me. I am "a danger to the public" because I have shot, killed and tortured a few members of the criminal world.

'If that's not Irish logic, I'm a Dutchman. You may as well charge rat catchers with being kidnappers as far as I'm concerned.'

'While Eddy was lying in the freezer for five days waiting for disposal, me and the Jew did another two other jobs of work. Busy, busy, busy. Ha, ha, ha.'

Fast Eddy

Fast Eddy got grabbed on a Friday night,
He dies on Sunday lunch,
I didn't use much violence,
I didn't kick or punch,
But we had some fun before he dies,
Yes we had some fun,
Played a game called kneecap,
Kneecap nail gun,
I had to keep Eddy fresh,
He spent five days in a fridge,
Until I could arrange his funeral,
Under West Gate Bridge,
Fast Eddy had a heap of gold,
And every ounce of it I sold,
Eddy had a heap of dash,
But not enough to keep his cash,
He made it all from selling dope,
But, in the end, he had no hope,
His mother wonders where Eddy is,
She cries and feels blue,
But don't cry, dear, this is just a poem,
And poems are rarely true.

'When I look back on the jelly beans I have shot, stabbed, bashed, iron-barred, axed, kneecapped, toe-cut, blowtorched, killed, and generally upended, I look at it like this: if I hadn't done it, then somebody else would have. I am not the only lion in the jungle, but I am the only one with no ears and a smiling face.'

On ambushing drug dealers
'They're like taxis. If you miss one another will be along shortly. And they both smell bad, too.'

'The crims today come from quite affluent backgrounds. It's shocking when you think about it. There is no excuse for some of them being inside. Some of them have matriculated and some have been to university. It's drugs that have got them here, you understand.'

'People want me to be Dirty Harry, cleaning up the world like a vigilante. I never said I was a hero. I robbed drug dealers because they had cash and couldn't complain. Steal your second-hand Commodore and you'll go to the cops. Steal twenty grand from a drug dealer and he keeps quiet. You do the sums.'

EVERYTHING ELSE

'In Tassie, there are three classes of criminals: white collar, blue collar and no collar.'

'I'd lived with murder contracts over my head for years.'

'Don't ask for mercy from a man who has been shown no mercy.'

'All I can do is put my best foot forward. But if, now and again, I put my best foot on the thick neck of some smartarse, that is not returning to crime, for God's sake.

'But just because the lion has left the jungle, it doesn't mean that he automatically turns into a monkey. I am what I am and I am who I am and I cannot and will not change my mental and emotional makeup. Walking away hasn't meant that I have gone through a personality reconstruction.'

'The screws joke with me about marrying into the landed gentry when they see the Jag-driving farmer's daughter come to visit. Ha ha.

'Grave digger I may be, but gold digger? Never.

'Mary-Ann has no brothers and only one sister and there were various crude jests about Mr Hodge not losing a daughter but gaining a Chopper, and at least I'd have plenty of room down on the farm to bury the bodies. (Memo to all authorities and potential in-laws... the bodies bit was a joke).'

'As with old football players, boxers and sportsmen, in any physical high-risk area, there comes a time to walk away. The ones who end up dead are mostly men who overstayed their time. When the barman yells "last orders" you leave, and I left.

'Had I stayed on I would have become more a figure of comedy than a figure of fear. There is nothing more embarrassing in my opinion than some over-the-hill old fart who still thinks he's a tough guy.'

'It's like a dog on a chain. You put the dog on the chain for the night then let him off the chain in the morning and he runs around and around the back yard like a raving nutter.

'You lock a man in a cage for a year or two or longer, then let him out, and you're going to be a sad girl if you think he's going to come home and sit in front of the telly with a tinny, 24 hours a day.

'When a bloke gets out of jail after a long stay he runs around like a mad rat, drinking all the piss, eating all the food and pinning tails to every donkey, or should I say ass, he can find.

'It doesn't mean you don't love the girl you have at home but it's like boiling water and having nowhere for the steam to go. Then one day the lid gets removed and something's got to blow.'

'It is 5.30am as I write this. I must let my chickens out and feed them and start my general duties on the farm. Paul Manning and I cut several tons of wood the other day and I think we have some other nice jobs lined up for today. It's either dipping sheep, drenching sheep, crutching sheep or shearing fucking sheep or bloody ploughing up the paddocks with the tractor… And to think I spent years fighting to get out of jail, to do this.

'Isn't that weird? I have seen men die, seen bodies, poured lime on the cold corpses of drug dealers who deserved to die and then stopped for a mixed grill on the way home, yum.

'But the sight of Big Gloria [the hen] dying while she fought for her chicks was too much for the old Chop.'

'As a city boy with simple tastes, I find the bush great fun. I've always been an adaptable fellow and I've quite taken to country life. Chainsawing the guts out of everything is great fun. It's nowhere near as good as turning up the heat on a drug dealer, but it's better than nude Twister.

'Trees are in their own way far more dangerous than drug dealers. Put the chainsaw to a drug dealer and they will wriggle and scream and beg and moan. They'll call to God and call their mates on the mobile phone and everything's sweet. But when you give it to a tree at night it can pay you back big time.

'One time under moonlight, I was giving a big gum the big lash when it paid me back. I had always believed that all things are based on logic. To me it seems perfectly logical to cut a tree down with a chainsaw at night by the light of the moon without being sure which way they may fall. It's sort of Russian Roulette with a giant hardwood.'

'They reckon you can outrun a tree – after all, it doesn't even have runners, but they keep coming very fast. And in the dark it's luck, either good or bad, on which way it falls. As I ran in the dark I knew that if I lived I would always remember the following three lessons…

'Lesson one: never cut a tree down at night;

'Lesson two: never cut a tree down at night when you are pissed;

'Lesson three: if you do cut a tree down at night when you are pissed, make sure the cool box is in a protected spot.'

'In the old days you'd just wave a chainsaw near a drug dealer and he'd put a grand in your hand just out of good manners. Now as a man of the land I am expected to work like a slave around the sheep shit and flies just to keep the wolf from the door.'

'Once, when he was young, Dad got the idea that the next-door neighbours were mistreating their family pet. Every time he looked over the fence the animal seemed to be getting thinner and thinner.

'He complained to the neighbours, and said he hated cruelty to animals. Every time he asked them if they were feeding the dog, they swore they were. But it seemed skinnier than ever, and one day Dad could take no more. He jumped the fence, threatened the neighbour with a beating, then took the dog and drowned it to put it out of its misery.

'It was the first time he had seen a greyhound.'

'If Jesus, the Son of God, came down to earth in the 20th century and walked the streets of Melbourne or Sydney, blessing people, healing the sick and turning water into wine, he would be arrested immediately and declared a crackpot.'

'Slip, slop, slap has been my motto. Slip on your shoes, slop some Irish whiskey into ya, and slap some lap-dancer on the arse.'

'Keep a mad person confused on a tight rope between anger and kindness and you keep him fascinated.'

'If you're quick on the uptake and able to read between the lines, the truth threads its way in and out of every yarn.

'It's like the bloke who is writing this book.

'He has got ears... you just can't see them.'

'You must remember I was in prison when political correctness crept up on the outside world, which makes me a member of some sort of deprived minority, when you think about it.'

'The more I see of people the more I like my dog.'

'It's like the monkey who roared like a lion at night and made all the animals in the jungle run away in panic and fear.

'The monkey started to think he was a lion because all the animals ran in fear of him at night. It was dark, none of the animals could see that the roaring monster was just a little monkey and so the monkey continued to rant and roar.

'Even the elephants ran away with the wolves and jackals, and the monkey roared out, "I am king of the jungle." Then one night the monkey came across a lion and the monkey roared and growled, but instead of running away in fear the lion charged forward and pounced on the monkey and tore him to shreds.

'In the morning all the animals came to look, and when they saw the dead monkey they all cried and asked the lion why he killed the poor monkey.

'The old lion looked at the dead monkey and, feeling a bit

puzzled himself, he said, "He's a dead monkey now, but last night he was a lion."

'I guess the moral is if you've got a banana in your hand you'd better eat it and stop waving it about trying to pretend it's a shotgun, and if you're a monkey stay in the trees and don't run around the jungle pretending to be a lion. If anybody wants to roar like lions, then they better make sure they have the teeth and claws to back it up. I for one have no tears for dead monkeys. The world is full of real dangers, and police are no different from any other people. When you hear the lion roar, you either fill it full of lead, or run like a rat. You certainly do not stop to check if it's a real one or you could end up dead. And I'm no police lover, I'm a lover of self-defence and I am a great believer in every human having a God-given right to self-defence.

'I reckon the jungle is becoming too full of monkeys who roar like lions, and when they die all that anyone sees, in hindsight, is the poor dead monkey and they all blame the poor old lion.

'I've shot a few of these roaring monkeys myself. Personally I can't stand the little bastards. Mind you, some of them gave me a few "gorillas" if I ever put my hand out. And some were more chumps than chimps.'

'Here is a story told to me as a small boy by my dear old dad, who was a sort of a bent Aussie version of Rudyard Kipling or Aesop.

'In relation to the equal division of funds, there is a yarn of the lion, the fox and the donkey who agree to form a partnership and go out hunting. They were the very best of comrades in arms and staunch and solid friends and plundered and killed with scant regard.

'At the end of their hunting adventure the lion told the donkey to share the proceeds out.

'The donkey divided the booty out into three equal parts, making sure to be extra careful and correct that each pile of goodies was exactly the same size and weight.

'When he was done, the donkey said to the lion, "You are king of the jungle so you have first pick."

'The lion said, "Thank you, my dear friend donkey." Then the lion looked at the three large piles of game, gold and goodies and all manner of good things to eat and he turned and sprang at the donkey in a fury and rage and killed and devoured him.

'When the lion had finished licking the donkey's blood from his claws, he looked at the terrified fox and said, "Dear old foxy, my fine fellow, would you be so good as to share out and divide the proceeds again in two piles. The donkey, bless his heart, won't be needing his."

'The cunning fox then set about collecting all the piles of goodies, gold and game and pushing it into one giant pile leaving only a few small left over tidbits in a very tiny pile for himself. Then the fox said, "Lion, my dear fellow, please take your pick."

'The lion looked at the tiny pile and then at the large pile and picked the large pile, then turned and said to the fox, "By the way, my dear foxy, who on earth taught you to share things out in such a manner?"

'"The donkey," replied the fox. Ha ha.'

'A philosopher is someone who points out the bleeding obvious to people who are too thick-headed to think of it themselves.'

'Good blokes are good blokes be they in the bush or in the city and a maggot is a maggot wherever you find him and the bush is no exception.

'However, when it's all said and done, where would I rather live? The bush or the city?

'The bush, of course. The snakes are just as deadly but they move a little slower.'

'A murder today is a tragic horror, but a murder yesterday is history and all men have a fascination with history.'

'I think my trouble is that I have become a bit of a sceptical old dinosaur. I've seen too much and I've become jaded and very suspicious. The world is changing and I don't seem to be changing with it… The whole nation is turning gay or green in a vomit of political correctness. I don't know whether to laugh, cry or shoot.'

'I'm not saying that a legend is nothing but a pack of lies. What I am saying is that one cannot create a legend without the help of a pack of lies. We start with some truth then add lies to build it up. Everyone adds another story to the story until we end up with a skyscraper of a legend. The lies are the glue that hold the whole thing together and as a result the lies within each and every legend are the most secret and protected part of the structure.'

'I have become philosophical about the old hand of fate, particularly when that hand is attached to some arthritic bureaucrat. They are all the same. They are stiffer than a body six hours in the boot. They are given a teaspoonful of power and they want to swing it round like a baseball bat. Oh well, never mind, it's all part of life's rich tapestry.

'A rooster one day, feather duster the next.'

'Most of the country people I've met could get work as trick knife tossers in any circus because sticking knives in people's backs is their favourite pastime.'

'It shows me that none of us can ever leave the past. It lies dormant in the back of our skulls and, like a dirty big wombat, comes out at night for a sniff around and a scratch.'

'With the entire human race dancing on the edge of its own grave, who gives a rat's about a few bottom bandits.'

'I received yet another phone call from the movie people wanting me to sign yet another contract. I've taken a few contracts in my time but nothing like the one the movie people keep running past me.'

'The funny thing about rope is that if you give people enough of it they insist on hanging themselves, and my smiling face and readiness to agree to the most insane arrangements is not politeness; it's rope.'

'The lawyers were paid more than a grand a day. I got a cheese sandwich.'

'In those days Alphonse should have laid off the cake, but what does it matter? Cholesterol didn't kill him, unless the mate who later shot him blew him away with eight cheeseburgers in the back.'

'When a man can admit to himself and others that the world is full of men, twice his size, who could beat him in a fight, then he is well on the way to never being beaten. I learned that a long time ago.'

'It's easy to separate the real psychos from the false pretenders. Art imitates life and within the criminal world life can also imitate art. It is a stage full of actors. The separation of fact from fiction is almost impossible. Pretenders and role players walk hand in hand with true-blue psychopaths.

'The difference is that the real psychopath lives in a world all of his own, deep in his own mind. The psycho may very well enjoy the company of actors and role players provided that the psychopath can join in on a drama created by the play actors in a theatre funded by drug dollars.

'The psychopath only wants to take part for his own comic reasons no matter if the game is true or false, created by real men of dream merchants. It is of no importance to the psychopath. He doesn't need to rehearse his lines in the play because he is not acting.'

'Let's kill all the lawyers.

'A wealthy man called his three best friends to his deathbed. They were a doctor, a politician and a lawyer. He told each man he wanted to take his money with him when he died. He then gave each man a million dollars and made each man swear to toss the money into his grave after the funeral.

'Afterwards, the doctor asked the politician, "Did you toss in all the money?"

'"Well, not quite," replied the politician. "I needed half a million for my re-election campaign and a further two hundred thousand for the new medical wing that is being named after me but I did toss in a hundred thousand. I'm sure the good lord and the dear departed will understand."

'"Yes," said the doctor. "Speaking of medical wings, I donated half a million to the medical research unit being named after me and I'm afraid I bought a new car and new house."

'"So how much did you toss into the grave?" asked the politician.

'The doctor, looking embarrassed, said, "Seventy-five thousand."

'The lawyer, listening in silence, shook his head in disgust. "Gentlemen, I'm ashamed of the both of you. I simply cannot believe what I'm hearing," said the lawyer.

'The doctor and politician both looked at the lawyer and spoke at once. "How much did you toss in then?" they asked.

'The lawyer held his head up and with a note of pride in his voice said, "Needless to say, gentlemen, I tossed in a cheque for the full amount."

'It's an old joke but it holds true today.

'When a lawyer does you a favour look close, count all your fingers after shaking his hand and kiss your money goodbye. Oh, and don't forget to thank him afterwards. I've sat in a lot of courtrooms and I haven't met one lawyer who hasn't tried to talk to me like I'm a mental retard. Criminal lawyers spend most of their time talking to criminals and most criminals are mental retards, therefore the lawyer does develop a superiority complex. It's an occupational hazard, I suppose.'

'You can talk about slamming someone's knob in a car door, shooting some wombat in the gut, or removing some sucker's toes with a blowtorch and that is considered the height of good humour, but mention that someone is a bit on the dusky side and you'll get ten years from the politically correct police.'

'There are some animals in the criminal world who would sell their wife on the streets to buy bullets and teach their kids to steal so Dad can drink the money. Ridding a family of such a man is, to my mind, an act of charity.'

'I had nothing against him personally, but he made his move and lost. In the chess game of life and death, you only get one move.'
'Freddy is a thickset, broad-shouldered, barrel-chested man with the physical strength of a small bull – and the courage of a rice bubble.'

'If the Mafia is so tough, why don't they have a branch office in Belfast?'

'The psychiatrist and psychologist are God's gift to the mentally ill, proving that God does have a sense of humour.'

'The children of this nation are dying at a faster rate than the bloody trees. Wake up before it is too late.'
'Revenge is a dish best eaten cold, and it has no time limit.'

'If you mix a man with a big mouth and a gangster complex who couldn't punch his way through a lady's lace hanky, you end up with a coward who is eager to impress.'
'Popularity seems to be the pot of gold many people spend their whole lives searching for.

'I have never bothered to try and look for popularity. Being hated, being unpopular, is safer ground. If you seek popularity, you will generally fail, ending up a pathetic figure of scorn and ridicule. You can even destroy yourself in the process. But men who are hated can actually gain a following of loyal admirers, while some who seek popularity end up being disliked and hated. These are people who won't stand up for what they believe in, but act only to be liked by others. People end up seeing through them.

'It is a confusing psychological topic. It is strange because I have received mail from people who reckon I'm great, because I'm the biggest arsehole they have ever heard of. So you figure it out.'

'There are other prison officers here who like to think they are heavy thinkers. One of them loves to sit down with me and have huge psychological debates about the pros and cons of the human mind. He has locked me into some debates, which have left me in dire need of a Panadol and a good lie down.

'He likes to climb inside your head and pick, pick, pick at your brain. My method is more likely to creep up behind you and go whack, whack, whack with an ice-pick.'

'We are all in search of the Holy Grail, the ultimate truth, the meaning of life. If God came down to earth and we all sat at his feet and asked, "Lord, tell us the answer," he would say, "Piss off, I'm trying to find where I came from."'

'This personal stupid, blind courage of honest men outweighs the personal courage of bad men. Why? Because bad men hold very little dear to their heart, whereas the honest man will often risk life and limb fighting with an intruder over a bloody television set or video.'

'I've got enough heavy-duty firepower and ammo stored

away to hold off a small army for three months. I believe that, when Australia is invaded, those who are not prepared will die... but the buggers won't get me without a fight.'

'Instead of ranting and raving, rolling about and sooking at the injustice of it all, I simply look at it this way: it is never checkmate until I'm dead; until then, it is just another move on the board.

'They make their move, I make mine. I don't take it personally and I hope they don't either.

'By getting angry I would lose my edge. Wars are won by men who are willing to fight them for a long time.'

'I am a man with a long, long memory. Shallow people and false pretenders don't have long memories. They will forget, but I won't. I don't have to shoot people to punish them. There are more easy ways to kill a cat than by wringing its neck. The cats in question used up their nine lives when they betrayed my trust and friendship, let me tell you.'

Sense of Humour

The mail came today,
One letter had a lot to say,
Tearful crying across the page,
A message of puzzled rage,
What, where, how and why,
Great concern that he would die,
Asking me if I was the offender,

Or the victim of a false pretender.
An angry young lady writing a letter,
It seems someone got hit with a 9mm Beretta,
I never replied. What's to be said?
No sense of humour, nobody's dead.

Chopper's thoughts on hitman Andrew Veniamin, who was shot dead by Carlton identity Mick Gatto in a Carlton restaurant. (Gatto was charged with murder but was acquitted on the grounds of self-defence.)

'Andrew lost the plot – so they put him in one.'

'A good big man will always shoot a good little one.

'Little Benji was silly to try and pick on a giant like Mick Gatto – of course it was a clear-cut case of self-defence. Thank God for juries.'

'They were only two men there. One said what happened and the other was dead. Who was going to argue it wasn't self-defence?'

'Mick was a heavyweight fighter. Veniamin was the size of a jockey. Gatto didn't need to shoot him. He could have sat on him.'

ON CHOPPER, THE MOVIE

'Eric Bana will go on and on to bigger and better projects. You don't have to be a fortune teller to predict that but I'd keep my eye on Vince Colosimo.

'Anyway, that's my prediction for what its worth. As for Eric Bana, what can I say? I can only repeat the old story about Elvis Presley entering an Elvis look-alike contest and coming third. Bana looked more like me in that movie than I did. Like I said to a local newspaper, had the role called for Eric to wear a dress he would have won Best Actress as well. That's how good an actor he is.'

'Eric Bana does a better Chopper than me.'

'I wanted Bana to do a sequel but he said he thought it would damage his career. I wrote to him to remind him that George Lazenby knocked back a second James Bond movie because he didn't want to be typecast. Good move, that.'

'I was signing some autographs for some Aboriginal kids in the outback and they asked me to use my real name – "Eric Bana". I thought it was me who spent more than twenty years in jail and had my ears cut off. I must be mistaken.'

'It was the Australian film industry's night of nights. They all got dressed up in their best clothes and just couldn't wait to be seen – and that was just the cocaine dealers.

'The starlets went to the hairdressers, the dress makers and the plastic surgeons. The blokes put on their tuxes and put socks in their undies so they looked like studs.

'They all practised their surprised looks in case they won. They rehearsed their speeches so they could say they hadn't prepared anything to say.

'Most of them now have tatts and drug habits yet they never do jail time. Work that out.

'For months, I would skip to the letter box hoping for an invitation to the night. I thought I could go as Eric Bana's date but they obviously forgot my address. For a while I thought of going and impersonating Eric like he had done to me. Would they have noticed?

'Who knows?

'I decided to watch it from home in Tassie. They put on their tailored suits. I put on my K-Mart tracksuit. They grazed on sushi. I watched the cattle graze and ate nine steamed dimmies (hope I didn't know anyone who went in them). They snorted some crack and coke. I cracked a Bundy and Coke.

'Still, it was a good night and I was happy that the crew from *Chopper* did well. So they bloody should have – they had a great subject to work with.

'Eric Bana won Best Actor, Simon Lyndon won Best Supporting Actor and 'Doctor Strangelove' Andrew Dominik won Best Director. Michele Bennett did not win Best Producer for the Best Movie. Pity, she deserved it.

'They gave the Best Movie to the Barbie doll film *Looking for a Bottle of Brandy* or some such forgettable stupid name. Who did she ever kill?'

Tony Mokbel: he ran but he couldn't hide.

Lewis Moran: good pickpocket, killed by cheap beer.

Roger: a tough old dog for a hard old road.

'Benji' Veniamin: Proof that you should beware Greeks offering lifts.

Big Mick: talks softly, carries a big stick … a shooting stick.

RIP Munster: Graham Kinniburgh's funeral.

Livelier times: The Munster didn't deserve to die.

Jason Moran: A wobbly-bottomed wombat who put holes in his manners too often.

Alphonse: Put holes in his manners with serious Italian people. His death did not surprise some.

Mario Condello: smart, but not as much as he thought.

Victor Peirce: best of a bad lot. Paternity unknown.

Judy Moran: banned from the Brunswick club for life.

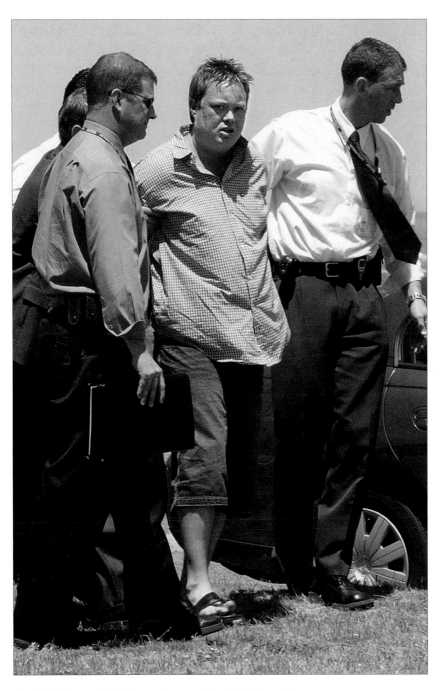

Carl Williams: A fat boy who got ahead of himself.

Class of '65 at Mornington State: I'm next to the fat kid with glasses in the middle row. But guess which side?

Zarah Garde-Wilson: My lawyer Bernie 'The Attorney' Balmer has a similar chest size, but that's where the resemblance ends.

When Eric won the best actor he said in his speech: 'I'd like to, ah, finally, of course, thank the two greatest casting directors in the world – Greg Apps and, of course, Mark Brandon Read. Thank you so much to the members of the AFI. I love this. Thank you… I can't cry because Chopper would be most disappointed.'

'The movie was big in Japan. The books have been translated into Polish and I am a cult figure in Canada. Only where mindless violence is applauded am I given my full credit. I could be a Tokyo Shock Jock except even I will baulk at eating raw fish.'

'The Polish translator wanted to know what this Australian expression "Esky" meant – did it mean "boat". I suppose it does as most of our hopes and dreams sail in them. The SS Crown Lager was my favourite before I had to give up the grog due to my rooted liver.'

Read has discovered that he is an artist, and his paintings selling around the world for around $5000.

'What I am doing isn't illegal but it is certainly bloody criminal.'

'I'd do this until the day I die.'

'I used to paint myself into a corner, now I've painted my way out of one.'

'The circus continues.'

'It takes me about two hours to do a painting that sells for six grand. If I knew that was the deal I would have gone straight years ago.'

'It is easier to clean up the mess from oil paints than after separating a drug dealer from his toes with bolt-cutters.'

'I'm a graphic artist. Very fucking graphic.'

Read's new reputation was sealed in 2003 at his first exhibition at Fitzroy gallery Dante's. Fans, the voyeuristic and collectors looking for good resale value snapped up all forty-five pieces. The State Library of Victoria purchased a Read self-portrait for $1400.

Sydney artist Adam Cullen, now a close friend of Read, inspired the former standover man when he sat for Cullen's entry in the 2002 Archibald Prize.

'I saw his stuff on the wall, and I said to him, "How much do you charge for this?"'

'He said, "I've just sold two to Elton John for $25,000 each."'

'I thought to myself, "How long's this shit been going on?" So I got hold of some acrylic paints and a brush and took it up.'

'Adam Cullen described it as post-modernist, neo-surrealist rubbish. It looks good up on walls, goes up in price, and fits good into the back of a BMW.'

CHOPPER ON THE MEDIA

'They tell me I shouldn't profit from crime — then they ring me up for an interview. Funny thing is they get paid for it. I don't.'

'At my wedding I had old crooks, loyal friends, family and a table of reporters. On each table was a bottle of Johnny Walker Black and Absolute Vodka. The reporters drank more than everyone else and then stole the booze on the way out. And they are the moral conscience of the nation. Go figure.'

'TV reporters try and beat me up on camera and then want an autograph after. And they call me a conman.'

'The gunnies from the Wild West that are famous aren't those that were the fastest on the draw. They were the ones who teamed up with the drunken reporters from the penny dreadfuls.'

'Not all the dangerous men get talked about in the newspapers or end up in courtrooms or prison cells.'

'Some of these so-called experts make me laugh. They are a veritable font of knowledge. They wouldn't know what they are talking about. They wouldn't know a crook of they woke up to find Marlon Brando trying to put a horse's head in their bed.'

'Derryn Hinch and me have a lot in common. Our livers are shot and we both like shooting at easy targets.'

'Alan Jones and me are no longer on speaking terms. He had a go at me and seemed hurt when I recalled he was involved in a misunderstanding with a policeman in a public toilet in London. Men in glass toilets shouldn't throw gallstones.'

'Come to think of it, there's an opening here for a good gunman to do strategic wounding of celebrities who can't cut the mustard any more. Think of the press coverage the occasional well-placed bullet would get.'

ON THE SOAP BOX

'A man has to know when to leave the party. If I had stayed, I would be dead. Jason and Mark Moran, Alphonse Gangitano – they couldn't hear the barman call last drinks. For them it was the *Last Post*.'

'I am deeply ashamed if my use of a blowtorch on drug dealers has had any lasting environmental impacts.'

'We have thousands of prisoners sitting around in million-dollar jails planning their next crimes and going out of their minds with boredom. Instead of having them sitting on psychiatrist couches telling lies, let's go back to the old-fashioned road gangs. Get them out in the bush. You want an irrigation pipe from Queensland to Victoria? You want trees planted along the way? Let's get half the junkies in jail out in the fresh air and sweat the poisons out of them. Have we forgotten half the main roads in Australia were built with convict labour? – signed Chopper Read, unemployed.'

'Terrorism, whether it be political or criminal, rarely achieves what people hope it will. It normally is a massive failure. The IRA has been blasting the hell out of the British for years and all it has achieved is to make the Brits more determined to dig in. The same with the PLO with the Israelis. The harder one side pushes the more the other one digs in.

'In Australia, we have had the Hilton and Russell Street bombings and the shooting of two policemen in Walsh Street. All three acts can be classed as terrorism and what did they achieve? They only strengthened the resolve of the politicians, police and the public. The immediate response is to give the police more funds and power. It strengthens the resolve of the police and bonds them together. If anything, it makes the police a tougher enemy.

'It seems to me that terrorism is a weapon of anger and not of intelligence.

'As I have stated before, to me revenge is a holy duty. It is not something to be loudmouthed about in pubs, or to big-note about. It is not just something that "should be done", but something that "must be done". In some way, either by my own hand or by my hand guiding the hand of another, I have always had my revenge. In the revenge department I see myself as something of a puppet master. I didn't kill Alex Tsakmakis, but he is dead.

'The use of terror tactics by criminals against criminals works a treat. It is an underground war where people like me can succeed. But using terror against the people, or the police protecting the people, political targets or any of the armed services, simply won't work.

'The only time terrorism works is when the target has no moral outrage. The Jews used terror to kick the Brits out of Palestine, but the Brits needed Palestine like a hole in the head. Terrorism may work against an enemy who believes he is in the wrong, but it will never work against an enemy who believes he is in the right.

'Righteous indignation takes over and no force on earth can defeat that.

'Terrorism defeats itself when it creates outrage in its victims.'

'It seems to me that the modern political scene is bullied and pushed, if not at times controlled, by small lobby groups. They are made up of blinkered people convinced that their single-interest issue is the most important thing in the world.

'There are the Greens, Greenpeace, Save the Whales and hundreds of other environmentally friendly, boring groups. You also have various ethnic lobby groups, sex groups, professional interest groups and sundry others. There must be hundreds of whacked-out nutters who have formed their own action factions.

'Meanwhile, the Japs are buying every square foot of land

they can get hold of and Vietnam has taken over major parts of Australia without firing a shot or digging a single tunnel.

'While the greenies are saving our wildlife, forests and waterways, our children are dying in the gutters and back alleys of the nation of drug addiction.

'While the gay lobby is fighting hard for their political rights, and the various women's groups are kicking up a storm, children are hocking their bums and fannies in the brothels, massage parlours and escort services of the country.

'There are plenty of lobby groups prepared to march in the street to save albino water fowl yet no one seems to utter a word of outrage that a generation of Australian children is being destroyed by drugs. No one seems to care about what really matters. Wake up before it is too late.

'Dad said, "Remember that, son. If ya ever need to "sneak go" a dago, ya can always get the bastards while they are having dinner. The buggers take all day. I can't stand these bastards who play with their food.

'"There are three sorts of people who dilly dally at the dinner table, son... wogs, poofters and members of the royal family."'

'The more I see the way poor old Aussieland is going, the madder I become. I grew up as a good little racist under the white Australia policy and, like every other red-blooded Aussie kid of that era, enjoyed putting a goodly bit of comical shit on the Abos, spooks, coons, slopes, chows, dagos, spags, spics, greasers and wogs – and whatever other third-world gin jockey or porch monkey that came along. And what bloody good fun it was.

'Yet the same Aussie kids would put shit on the Germans for what they did to the Jews and we always enjoyed hating the filthy Japs for what they did to the Diggers during the Second World War.

'We all grew up racist but we picked and chose. There were exceptions and contradictions to our racist rules and all in the name of fun. We would put shit on the Abos, yet jump to their defence if any outsider such as some wog tried to put shit on what was after all the real Australian. We were, and still are, a confused lot of buggers indeed.

'Australia has no religious hatreds apart from the fact that everyone's dad was either a Catholic or a Freemason. We would happily put shit on every wog in town, except of course for the Italian and Greek kids we classed as our friends, because they weren't wogs, they were our mates.

'The wogs were the buggers from the next suburb we fought with on Saturday night.

'As far as our racist attitudes went, we invented the rules as we went along, making exceptions for friends and allowing all sorts of contradictions to our elastic rules. I guess you could say that our racist attitude was a rule of law that we applied nine out of ten times. Sporting identities, boxers, footy players and wog chicks with big tits were the general exceptions, and our friends of the non-Australian variety.'

'The criminal world is multiculturalism's showcase. Here crims don't care where you're from only if you can do the business. Here a fat white boy may use a Lebo hitman to go after an Italian. A Viet drug importer may sell his heroin to an Aussie trafficker in a Chinese restaurant. A Mafia wiseguy might go to the footy with his Aussie-born lawyer. A Turkish standover man may end up in a dim sim machine after he has punched a hole in his manners. And they all want an American Express platinum card. The criminal world is one big glorious melting pot. Al Grassby would be pleased if he wasn't dead, which means he's probably lost interest.'

'The Sicilians will threaten to kill your mother. The Vietnamese really will kill your mother. However, the Albanian Mafia will actually not only kill your mother but put the body in the cooking pot. The KGB didn't use the Albanians as hitmen for nothing. Next to the Irish, they would be the greatest mental cases in the criminal world.

'Ever wondered why there's no Mafia in Ireland?'

'My own view is that the Middle Eastern political groups are wolves dressed in sheep's clothing. I suspect they have a hidden agenda.'

'The Asians' taste for blood is a tad greater than those who control the areas at the moment… killing the family of an enemy is part of the Asian criminal culture. That's one reason why I would say the little chaps will climb right to the top of the criminal ladder.'

'The Italians changed the face of the criminal world in Australia in the 1960s with the Mafia and the "black hand" murders in the Melbourne markets. I'll give the rice eaters until the year 2000. By then, mainstream criminals, including the Italians, who have not come to some form of friendly agreement or understanding with these evil little men will have to make their own arrangements, with one eye in the back of their heads.'

'The Jap crims are the subject of some interesting chat. One fellow I know, a top crim, has told me personally that the first Jap he sees with tattoos or a missing finger, he will cut his head off and put it in a pickle jar.

'Where is the logic, you ask? That's why the head-hunter and blood merchants can't be beaten. There is no logic. You ask why. I say, "Why not?" The head-hunters and blood merchants, though few in numbers, could be seen as a criminal version of pest control. Criminally speaking we'll put up with the wogs and tolerate the Vietnamese – but we are not going to cop the bloody Japs, let me tell you.

'But the Vietnamese will keep coming back, and, if they get hold of the right killing weapons, there will be bodies dropping.

'I'd rather be backed up by one hated arsehole who can stick fat than a hundred popular show ponies who can't keep their mouths shut. I can name a lot of crooks, including myself, who could turn around tomorrow and say I know where the body is buried or I know who did it, just to get out of jail. Traitors are shot in wartime, but in peacetime they are encouraged and protected.

'The great Australian moral code is a thing of the past.'

The Fairy Gangsters

If the Mafia had a comedy,
Then Melbourne's the song they'd sing,
Led by buttercup Vito,
Who likes to be the King,
He looks like a million dollars,
In slip-on shoes and shirt,
And rumour has it, after hours, he slips on a lady's skirt,
He carries a gun just for fun, and keeps money in his shoe,
So if you're hunting for his wallet, I think the rumour's true,
And with his gang of hangers-on, they look a funny sight,
They love to bag The Chopper, every day and night,
They get down to the two-up, where they love to stand and meet,
The two-bob fairy gangsters,
The crew from Lygon Street.

'There are bludgers around this great country who have jumped on the Abo welfare gravy train claiming they are part of some tribe or another. They think that, because their great-great-grandfathers once waved at Truganini from a distance of 300 yards, they can claim Aboriginal descent and jump on the welfare bus.

'If you have feathers and webbed feet, if you swim in water and go quack, quack and look like a duck then it's a safe bet you're a bloody duck, it doesn't matter if your great-great-grandfather was a bloody budgie. If you have white skin and blond or red hair or any colour hair, for that matter, then you're white. It's no use trying to say you're a black man.

'I reckon the Aussie Abo is a good bloke and good luck to him. It's these white false pretenders that create all the trouble. I'm not dirty on the poor old dinky-di Abos. I don't think any Aussie is, but I am a bit dirty on the snow-white "Koori" fakes who on the strength of nothing, or a teaspoon of Aboriginal blood a hundred years back, expect the Aussie taxpayer to wipe their backsides for them for the rest of their lives. The whole thing has got out of hand. The whiter they get, the more they bloody want. They're as bad as the bloody public servants.'

PRISON LIFE

In August 1994, the Victorian Government finally closed the most notorious section of the prison system, H Division.

'The modern prison is a marshmallow compared with good old H. It was the last place from the old hard school and in my heart I preferred the old days to the system that we have now. A good flogging can concentrate the mind.

'I did more than ten years in "H", the so-called blood house of the system. It wasn't just my home, I owned the place.

'I owned it, I controlled it, I ran it. By ruling that division, we ran the jail. We were the most feared gang in the most feared division of the most feared jail in Australia, and I was the commanding general.

'I ran a five-year gang war from within the walls of H Division. And we had the power and influence to reach out from behind those walls.'

'It was the place where we made our own rules. I used all my tactical and strategic expertise. My rule was total and without question. I put together a crew of nutters never before seen in any prison, and we waged a prison war, which went on for years.

'It was the sort of violence that only ever existed in war. God, I loved it. It is the gang war, which is now part of Victorian jail legend.'

'If you are a police informer or an offender against small children, you can buy yourself all the friends and supporters you want with a gram of heroin. Not like the old days when a child molester could look forward to having a mop inserted in his bottom and then be flogged to within an inch of his pathetic life.'

'Police informers, crown witnesses, child killers and molesters openly running about the jails of the nation without a care in the world, and some of them swaggering about like gangsters… it's enough to make you sick.'

'"If you cannot kill the one you want then kill the one you are with", as the tattoo on my back says, but those days are gone now. I just sit with my cup of tea and watch the passing parade and smile to myself. Mind you, it's just possible that the occasional child molester could still have an accident. I'm a firm believer that there is a God, and that some of us have to do God's work.'

'Jail is full of blokes with plans to beat the system.'

'Most escape plots are hatched out of boredom. Prisoners want something to keep them interested. When you have people spending all their waking hours thinking about something, they end up finding an answer. That is why there is no such thing as an escape-proof jail. If the human mind is capable of designing and building it, the human mind is capable of beating it.'

'I was never a big escaper, preferring to do my time and amuse myself with wars inside the prison walls. The only time I tried to escape, it was a disaster.'

'I do time easier than most because I've learned to go with the flow. I observe people and learn to find the best in them. Those who fight jail end up being destroyed by it.'

'The biggest thing I miss in jail – apart from sex, guns, and Irish whiskey – is gambling. Roulette in particular.'

'Basically, it works like this. If I want an extra bit of toast or butter or permission to get a pair of sunglasses sent in, or a gold cross and chain, or a pair of runners or a contact visit, I go to the Governor of the prison. But anything larger than a contact visit and I have to get down on my knees and call on divine intervention as the Governor is powerless to help. He has the power to punish but his power to grant requests is limited.'

'You need more than a legal degree to be a lawyer. You need to care, because you're dealing with men and women in trouble. Guilty or innocent, these poor buggers are at their wits' end. Some are on the edge of suicide or, at best, a nervous breakdown.

'The remand yard of a prison is a cold and lonely place, and your lawyer for that period in your life is your only true friend, and my advice to any who seek it is to pick your friends wisely.'

'Don't do what I have done; it is a mess and a one-way road to disaster. You cannot take on the world, drug bosses, police, gangsters and the courts. If one doesn't get you, one of the others will.

'Go straight, young man. It may sound boring but, in the long run, it is the way to go.'

'In Australia, it is considered perfectly wonderful to talk at length about what you would like to do, and providing you never do it no man will raise his voice against you. But, if you get off your arse and get out there and actually do it, the critics will knock you.

'Criminals are told to pick themselves up, dust themselves

off, and improve themselves. But the very, very few who have tried to do just that are widely condemned.

'Criminals are told to mend their ways and improve themselves, but, when we do, the rules get changed. The people who run the game not only have the umpires in their pocket, but they move the bloody goalposts halfway through the match. How can you win?'

'On the wall behind the three Supreme Court judges is the Tasmanian coat of arms. There is a large wooden lion on the right-hand side and a unicorn on the left. Both are rising up on their hind legs, guarding some sort of smaller coat of arms in the shape of a shield, under this are the Latin words DIEU ET MON DROIT.

'I don't know what it means, but, if some of the numb-nuts sitting in the back of the court are any indication, it should read: "Thalidomide: yum, yum, we love it".'

'Ahh, it's a great life. What a bloody disaster.'

'Apparently, the crusaders down here have been taking my name in vain and suggesting I would be first cab off the rank. I have heard reports they intend to take the money I made out of my books and declare that it was made from crime. Well, good luck to them. If they saw my legal bills over this latest fiasco, they would realise that I would have to write the *Encyclopaedia Britannica* to even break even.'

'I'd rather have a lawyer shake your hand with the slight odour of Canadian Club Whisky about his person than reeking of Chanel No 5. I have met my fair share of (how can I say this politely?) screaming queens in the legal profession.'

'Only mugs and poor sports blame their bloody lawyers.'

'If God loves a sinner, he must really love me.'

'I know there are people who would be as delighted as a pack of poofters in a Vaseline factory if I shut up and stayed in jail. But I will not be silenced. I remain the greatest living writer with no ears in the world.

'Such is life.

'You'd have to be Linda Lovelace to swallow all that.'

The Last Word?

So now you've read my third book,
It really should be the last,
For a bloke who can't spell too good,
I write the buggers fast.
But maybe in time to come,
When I've got more to tell,
I might just take pen in hand,
And give the numb-nuts hell.
But for now, I'll wave goodbye,
And quietly fade away,
Writing gives me a headache,
And I'm calling it a day.
But if the legal bills keep mounting,

And you really do want more,
Bugger it, what the hell?
I might write Chopper Four.
Ha ha.

ON LIFE

'With the entire human race dancing on the edge of its own grave, who gives a rat's about a few bottom bandits.'

'I have found in the past that lethal weapons tend to get opponents to see the logic of your argument.'

'The fact is, no man can spend his whole life trying to be a tough guy. Sooner or later you've got to try in some small way to behave in some sort of normal manner by talking to normal people – as opposed to cops, robbers and lawyers, who definitely aren't normal.'

'I was once attacked by a crazy Greek wielding a plastic rubbish bin and I was holding a sawn-off shotgun. People flip out when they think they are in a corner.'

ON CHOPPER

'You don't get a reputation like mine for being a nice guy.'

'When it comes to violence, Chopper wrote the book.'

'Personally I would rather shoot someone than go through

the messy business of fighting them. But in jail it is anything from bare fists to razor blades, butcher's knives to iron bars. To stand on top of the heap for twenty years simply means you are more frightened of death than the other fellow.

'I don't fight to win, I fight to kill, so even if I don't kill I win. No crim could survive the baggings I've got. The only reason I am still around is because I can fight like a death adder. But I know my limitations; I know that after twenty years I am not as strong or as big as I once was.'

'I go out of my way to avoid three things: manual labour, physical exercise and fisticuffs. While others engage in all manner of combat training, pumping iron, punching bags, kicking each other, huffing and puffing and sweating like pigs in an effort to build themselves into fighting machines, I prefer to avoid all that hard work.'

'I do all my fighting with a gun in one hand and a cup of tea in the other. While the world is full of people who could bash me, the world is not full of people who could bash me and live to talk about it. That's why God invented razor blades, butcher's knives, iron bars, meat axes and guns that go bang – so blokes like me don't get bashed ten times a day before breakfast.'

'In the end, the secret to everything is to think like a rattlesnake and smile like a used-car salesman. And, for goodness sake, don't get that piece of advice the wrong way around. Be polite, be friendly, be non-aggressive, see trouble and avoid it, but, if trouble forces itself upon you, strike first and strike hard, just like a rattlesnake.'

'You are not a coward because you feel fear. It is there to stop us tongue-kissing tiger snakes. It has its natural place, but it must never be allowed to cloud the mind. I have seen people crippled with fear for no logical reason. And the person who does not understand his own fear cannot use fear against others.'

'My reputation in the criminal world has always been based on other people's hatred, fear and paranoia. My image has been made by my enemies, whereas a host of big-name crooks have reputations which come from their friends, admirers and hangers-on.'

'I fell out with Dennis Allen the way I have fallen out with most people... I belted him.'

'He used to talk so much about all the violence it went in one ear and out the other. Or so to speak... I don't have any ears.'

'Those who know me well will tell you I love a bit of a debate, although they might also say I like to finish the discussion with a baseball bat or a blowtorch. I have found in the past that lethal weapons tend to get opponents to see the logic of your argument.'

'Maybe it's some sort of midlife crisis. Once I used to think I was immortal; now it's suddenly hit me that I'm not. Bloody hell. It's a shock when you approach forty and find yourself sitting in a prison cell, realising you have spent nearly twenty of those forty years behind bars. What a waste.

'Even as a kid I was always a bit of a backyard philosopher. In those days, I always believed that the cornerstone of all correct thinking was that good will conquer evil. But as you get older you learn that evil built the world, and, when the so-called great and good men of history wished to achieve great and good things, they did not hesitate to walk over the bodies of millions of people to achieve their ends.

'So what is good and what is evil? It's all a psychological blur. When a private individual kills a few people, he or she is a monster. But when a politician kills a few million, he goes down in history as a man of great vision.'

'I personally wouldn't have the bad manners to put anybody in a boot – alive that is. It'd be far too uncomfortable for that.'

'There is not a gunman alive who frightens me, but I became terrified of people in shops, especially of fat ladies in lambswool slippers. They would scream out, "Look, that's the bloke on the telly. He's a murderer."

'Call me sensitive, but I couldn't cop that.'

'I would relieve any man of his heart and lungs with a double-barrelled shotgun if he tried to turn his hand against me or mine. In other words, hurt me or mine and I'll cut your ears off, put a hole in your manners and I'll rip your bloody nose off with a pair of multi-grips.'

'Not many people will believe this, particularly those that I have bashed, or had their feet warmed with the gas blowtorch, but I don't feel hate. I just don't know what it feels like. I mean, I can pretend to hate, but the most I can feel is to be a little cross with someone.'

'My attitude was that, if you don't carry your gun on you, you might as well not have a gun at all.'

'I swallowed my own top teeth years ago. They bloody nearly killed me going down and it was an uncomfortable experience getting them out the other end. Maybe that's why some people reckon I talk out of my arse.'

'If people want to try and bash me that's fine, as long as they don't mind spending the rest of their lives in a wheelchair or being led around by a seeing-eye dog.

'If they really want to rock and roll, then it would be a coffin for them. The only thing I get bashed with these days is bullshit. Shoot me, but, for goodness sake, don't shit me, as the old saying goes.'

'A bullet is the one thing which brings a man back to his real self. A truly hard man will remain hard, even after being shot. He will look you in the eye and say, do your worst. I've met a few tough bastards, but, believe me, they are rare.

'Just because a man has a few tattoos, a criminal record and a love of blood doesn't make him a hard man. There are some real weak men who hide their cowardice behind a gun and a tough image. And there are honest quiet men who, when pushed, have a touch of steel in their spines.

'Most so-called tough guys will cry and panic and get this pathetic childlike look when death stares them in the face. They plead and beg and whimper like puppies. They beg and cry for you to spare them.

'It is then that you see the real person behind the false face. I love it.'

'If anyone farts in my general direction, from a distance of 300 yards, they are in bother. Ha ha.'

'I was leading the mentally ill, but in my own way I was the worst of them all. I had the smiling face of a young angel, and a heart so full of tears that there was no room for the blood to flow. I was emotionally and mentally twisted. As a young guy I was cruel, cold and totally without human mercy, feeling or compassion.

'I didn't feel hate. I was just emotionally numb. All I had was my own sense of right and wrong. I saw everything only in terms of battles and strategies. I lived to spill the blood of enemies, and there were plenty of them.

'I am almost gentle and overflowing with human kind-ness when I look at myself now, compared with what I was.'

'Let's face it, I was as nutty as a fruitcake. Thank God, I'm all better now. Ha, ha, ha.'

'Why is it that every time I wave at a psychiatrist from a distance of 300 metres he tosses a handful of pills down my neck? ... They have just given me my nightly "bomb me out pill" and the white clouds are rolling in.'

'Chopper Read has left the stage and is just sitting in a chicken shed playing cards with Elvis. No guns allowed.'

'Have seen so much pain and suffering in my life. I have had people die in my arms and die at my hand. I thought I could not sink any lower but I was wrong. I have now been lowered into the abyss of hell. I have been banned from the only pub in town.'

'Then again, what would I know? I'm just a roaring drunk, a hopeless liar or a roaring liar and a hopeless drunk, or so some would have you believe.'

'I see myself as the typical Aussie male. Sure I may be covered in tattoos, have no ears, have a criminal record you can't jump over and torture drug dealers for profit and pleasure, but I personally see those as minor cosmetic differences. Underneath it all, I am just like the next bloke. I like a laugh, a drink, shooting scumbags and, most of all, when I am on the outside, I like a bet.'

'If people don't like me they can either kill me or cop it sweet, and until I am in my grave they can stick it as far as I'm concerned. To hell with them all.

'Their hatred is like sunshine to me. I thrive on it. There is something about me that seems to inflame hatred and passion in many people. I just don't understand it myself. To me I am just your everyday normal killer, but to others I seem to be the devil in disguise.'

'I am like a magnet to the mentally ill.'

'The truth is that I will never make enough money to buy anything for anybody. I have a team of lawyers to support. After all, charity begins at home.'

'I get mail from some people who see me as some sort of Robin Hood, a crusader who has set himself up to clean the world of drug dealers… I don't want people to get the wrong impression. I don't take from the rich and give to the poor. I keep the money myself. My life will never be made into a Disney movie. It is business. It is not and has never been some sort of holy crusade. But it can be fun, and quite profitable too.'

'I've been a crook for a long, long time, but, in my own way, I have been an honest crook. I will stand up and say, yes, I did that, and I did this, but I didn't do the other. I expect to be believed.

'Bloody hell, I can't be guilty of everything. Can I?'

'Well, a lot of people have described me as manipulating and cunning and that I always played the system and worked things to my advantage. Well, yes, yes. I did do just that. And anyone with half a brain would do exactly the same. If I was in politics, I'd be manipulative, cunning. I would work the system to my advantage. If I was in business, I'd be manipulative, cunning. I would work the system to my advantage. If I was in television, I'd be manipulative, cunning. I would work the system to my advantage. If I'm in jail, I'm manipulative, cunning, and I work the system to my advantage. You know, I was the organ grinder and they were the monkeys, and that's the way it worked.'

'As a teenager I was always interested in joining the army. I did try to enlist once but got knocked back because I failed the psychiatric test… the female captain psychiatrist said I had a personality given to violence.

'Using that as an excuse to stop someone joining the army – well, I thought it was quite amusing. I admit, I also had flat feet, but I didn't get as far as the medical.'

'In 1977 when I got out of prison, with my dad's help and on his advice, I applied to join the Rhodesian Security Forces. I wrote away to the head of the forces – Major General Kurt something or other. As I expected, I was accepted.

'I told the Parole Board via my parole officer that I was leaving. "No you aren't," said the parole officer. "You're on parole; you're going nowhere."

'Had I been allowed to leave we wouldn't be bothering with this now.'

'Some men dream of dying in a hail of bullets, and in 1977 I was one of those men.'

'Let's face it, the Australian crim isn't a great one for any form of gun-in-hand, face-to-face shoot-it-out combat. If they ever get me, it will be in the back.'

'I'm turning into that good man with a bit of a dark side instead of a bad man with a good side.'

ON AUSTRALIA

'The whole nation is turning gay or green in a vomit of political correctness. Everyone's torn up their Smokey Dawson membership cards and tossed them in the fire, half the country couldn't tell you who Banjo Paterson or Ned Kelly were, and the whole nation is steaming full steam ahead into the 21st century to the electric hip-hop beat of some Yankee Doodle basketball music… and I'm just walking backwards in the other direction "back down that track to an old-fashioned shack" to the Aussie land of my memory.'

'I like the Queen of England and the royal family, although a few of the younger ones could do with a blindfold and a last cigarette. The Queen herself is a lovely old dear, but she is the Queen of England, Scotland, Wales and Northern (in name only) Ireland. She is not the Queen of Aussie land. Well, she is, but no one really takes it seriously, outside the Melbourne Club.'

'Some of the young crims here think culture is something you make yoghurt with. They believe they can learn about Asian history by watching *Ninja Turtles*. They think Henry Lawson bowled for Australia, and Banjo Paterson's is a theatre restaurant in Adelaide.

'Can you believe that? Yet the same young men know the words off by heart to half the songs AC/DC ever wrote.

'Who was it who wrote *Poor Fellow My Country*? Xavier Herbert? Well, he wasn't far wrong, was he?

'The Americanisation of Australia seems to be the problem. The Yanks killed Phar Lap and Les Darcy and they have been trying to kill off everything Australian ever since. The buggers have nearly done it and I'm just as bloody guilty as everyone else for falling victim to it.

'This country has a great history and yet you wouldn't know it. The kids walk around with baseball hats on, shirts with gridiron teams' emblems on the front. They have pictures of American basketballers on their walls. They think Chips Rafferty invented the potato cake.

'We look up to Yankeeland heroes and look down on our own. It makes me bloody sick. Too much bloody television, if you ask me. It's killing us all. Kids should not be indoors watching television, they should be outside, punching on with their mates, getting a bit of fresh air and doing a bit of male bonding.

'Mind you, my distaste for America does not include Gary Cooper, John Wayne, Paul Newman and Edward G Robinson. God bless them all, the dirty rats.'

'Sydney may have all the razzle dazzle but most of the deadly serious work gets done in Melbourne. There is no doubt it is the unofficial murder capital of Australia.'

'Australia is a big country and shovels are cheap. Victoria may be the garden state but, if you dug it up, you would find a heap of bodies. The garden probably grows so well because of all the blood and bone that has been spread over it.

'If a crook goes missing in Melbourne chances are he isn't on holiday at Surfers Paradise. Anybody who adds up the numbers over the last 100 years will see I am right. Victoria is the state of the big vanish.'

Yankee Doodle Aussie
Yeah, they call it Aussie music,
With their Mississippi twang,
Singing down home Yankee songs,
With a touch of Aussie slang,
They sold out to Waylon Jennings,
And sing Rockabilly Blue,
But what they all forget
Is that Aussie land has its legends too,
Yeah, I know Tex Morton's dead,
And his songs are getting rusty,
But there's one Aussie Boy who won't die,
A legend named Slim Dusty,
And what about Banjo Paterson,
And a bloke named Henry Lawson,

Old Flash is dead and gone,
But we've still got Smokey Dawson,
They get up there to Tamworth,
With their Texas hats and bash,
But as far as I'm concerned,
They can jam their Johnny Cash,
Give me Waltzing Matilda,
And the Road to Gundagai,
Hell, I'd rather hear Chad Morgan scream,
Than Willie Nelson cry,
Did you know that Hank Williams died,
With a needle up his arm,
He was just a southern junkie,
And a long way from the farm,
So if you want to sing Aussie country,
And become a legend too,
Forget the Yankee Doodle shit,
And stick to Old True Blue.

A poem for legendary Tasmanian QC Michael Hodgeman

The Mouth from the South
From Queenstown to Hobart Town,
From Canberra to Darling Downs,
He's fought a thousand battles,
In a hundred different towns,
And while he's very sober,
And always in good condition,

He's a soap-box battler,
A dinkum Aussie politician,
And while most just call him Michael,
When they're drunk they call him Mick,
They know the Mouth from the South,
Will never miss a trick.
The champion of the underdog,
And the drinking man's friend,
He'll start a fight then finish it,
And take it to the end,
And when it comes to trouble, boy,
He don't ever run and hide,
And when your back's against the wall,
You'll find him at your side,
And when the Devil comes a knocking,
He'll stick there to the end,
And I'm proud I even shook his hand,
He's the Aussie battler's friend.

Read was charged with the murder of Sammy the Turk Ozerkam. He beat it on self-defence.

Sammy the Turk
She said get The Chopper out of the bar,
Shane and the boys are in the car,
If you help set up the Big Fella, Turk, you'll be a star,
The boys farmed it out, they got ghosted,
But as Sammy walked out the door, the boys just left him posted.

The game was for real, it was no lark,
But Sammy walked toward the wrong car park,
Silly boys, was all The Chopper had to say,
It wasn't their lucky day,
And poor Sammy the Turk got blown away.

Darcy

He sat on the bench,
For many years,
He gave us laughs,
And sometimes tears,
He had a way,
All his own,
And for style,
He stood alone,
With smiling face,
And big bow tie,
My word, he did look classy,
Every crook in Melbourne knew him,
The Magistrate called Darcy.

Sanity in Cell 37

In a world feeding on war and fear,
A world starving of love,
I watched a man drowning in blood and the tears,
Of a sick and dying dove,
A total enigma, a puzzle misunderstood,
Seen as evil in his attempts to do good,

234

They paid him in torment and emotional pain,
For trying to save us from nuclear rain,
And why, I asked, does he even care,
For a world that cares nothing for him,
Apathy, he answered, that's our greatest sin,
He spoke of a nuclear nightmare that will come upon us all,
It's just a question of time before our Rome will fall,
I read a bit about him and what he was meant to be,
Some said he was CIA, some said he was KGB,
The answer's there, the answer's clear,
But still they fail to see,
He screams words of sanity to the deaf, dumb and blind,
So they locked him away with the criminally ill,
But he's not one of our kind, nor is he a dill,
I see a rage within him others fail to see,
In his utter frustration and the knowledge he can't prevent what he
knows he will be,
The anti-nuclear warrior, or the monster from Death Heaven,
The nightmare prophet in cell 37.

A poem to Justice Frank Vincent who was also chairman of the Parole Board.

Big Frank
For classic courtroom comedy,
In Australia we are not short,
And the funniest of them all,
Sits in a Melbourne Court,

The Mick Irish son of a tough old dockie,
Heart of gold, but his head's a little rocky,
The Chairman of the Board,
As every crook will know,
They tried to pull his coat,
But he still let the Texan go,
He hits 'em in the courtroom,
Like an Irish tank,
The knockabout Judge,
They all call Big Frank.

Ha ha.
M.B.R.

CHAPTER 5

READ ON THE RECORD

11 April 1977

I request to be transferred into One Yard for protection because there are prisoners in this division that firmly believe that I bashed Bobby Barron on behalf of the prison officers. This is not true, but it is a very hard thing to disprove.

MARK BRANDON READ

Comments
Read has proved to be a standover type, his application is not recommended.

(They were right. I did bash Barron. But I did the prison service a favour. Bobby was a much more pleasant personality after I hit him with a spade.)

12 July 1977

To Mr H Poden, Parole officer, Head Office
Memorandum
Mark Read
File No 74/4480

The above named is scheduled to be released on parole some time next August and you have been assigned as his parole officer.

Best of British luck
R H Perch

Released from jail 1977

N L Doyle
FILE NOTE
74/4480

26 April 1976

Interviewed in G Division. He is to appear in court (St Kilda) tomorrow 27/4/78 on charges of assault. He does not know when his Supreme Court case is on.

Mark is in a quite jocular state, asking how much do I think he'll get for his offences. Explains he doesn't think he's done anything really serious. With regard to the assault, he claims that the man he attacked was a hoon and he deserved what he got, the police stood and watched him and agreed it was deserved. Mark feels he has done the community a service. Asked about his attempted

*abduction of Judge Martin, had he thought he could pull it off?
Says yes…*

*Asked about his ears: says decided he would do a 'Van Gogh',
needed to draw attention to himself drastically as wrists didn't
attract enough attention, 'everybody does that.' States that he got
Kevin Taylor to cut them off. He started to saw at one and then
Mark said, 'Don't saw, slash it off', which Taylor did. He then did
the same to the other one and then vomited. Mark under the
impression that you didn't lose much blood when you cut ears off
and was surprised to lose five pints. Also thought it could be sewn
back on again quite easily. Thought he might be declared insane
after this but when advised could end up a Governor's Pleasure
decided 'he couldn't win'.*

*Mark seems to want assurances that his offences are not really
serious, whilst inviting the prison officer to assure that they really
are extremely audacious and daring. No comments were elicited.*

*The relation of these offences by Read were done in a light
hearted and humorous fashion, which made it extremely difficult to
keep a straight face. However there is little doubt that Mark's
impetuosity is extremely dangerous. I do not think that anyone
would disagree that this lad is a true-blue psychopath. An earlier
diagnosis of autism is interesting, as is father's presentation.*

28 November 1978

The Superintendent
H. M. Prison, Pentridge
Self-inflicted injury on prisoner
Mark Read, H Division.

Sir,
On Monday, November 27, 1978 it was reported to me at
1.10pm by acting chief prison officer Hildebrand that H Division
prisoner, Mark Read had inflicted three slashes to his right cheek
with a razor blade...

Read said: 'Sir, I seem to have cut my face, could you get a medic,
with a couple of aspirins and a couple of bandaids'. I asked him if
he felt the wounds were serious and he replied: 'No Sir, a couple of
bandaids will do.'

PRISONER APPLICATION FOR
RECLASSIFICATION

Dear Sir,
I would rather not linger too long in this division or in Pentridge. I
would like to get to a nice, easygoing country jail and out of the
way altogether. So as soon as you think I've proved that I can live
peacefully with my fellow man or whenever you think you can talk
the Director General into it, I'd like to get the hell out of here.

I am very grateful for being given the chance to get out of Jika
and to come to J of all places.

I guess I feel like a man who has to keep changing trains to get the last one home. H was the start, G was a stop over, then back to H, then on to Jika Jika, now J Division.

I guess I won't really be able to relax in my mind until I am on the last train home when I can say right this is it, no more questioning and wondering. I guess after six years of maximum security divisions and my last sentence was mostly in H Division, with a bit of D and B Division tossed in, the J Division set is real fantasy land.

Since I have been in Pentridge, I have had a bad run with personal relationships, they come and go. If I get to a country jail and get a local guy who's doing time to put me on to a local girl and get visits every week. Jika messed up my last relationship and if I bother to try and get a new friend, she will only drop off when I get sent away. So I've got a few reasons for wanting to get to a nice country jail and do it easy.

Thank you very much.

PS: Beechworth sounds nice. Geelong is a dirty old hole. Thank you very much.

Mark Brandon Read, model prisoner and totally reformed.

Transferred to Geelong.

CLASSIFICATION ANNUAL REVIEW

Chief or senior prison officer's report:
No problem since he arrived at Geelong
Welfare Officer's Report:
Mark has been at Geelong for several months and appears to have settled in satisfactorily. He mixes little with other inmates with the exception of a select few. He makes few requests and no demands.

Governor's report:
Read has not encountered any problems since his arrival at Geelong. He is a deep-thinking type who keeps very much to himself. He needs supervision because of his record and his heavy medication. Recommended that he remain at Geelong. Review in December 1984.

MEMORANDUM

21 December 1984
Prisoner Read has been at Geelong since March 1984. His conduct on the surface has been excellent. Lately he has been receiving what he calls 'gifts from other prisoners'. He has never purchased a canteen, but is never without canteen items.

TRANSFER DETAILS

21 December

Prisoner's name: READ, Mark Brandon

Transfer details: To H Division

Reason for transfer: Suspected of standing over other prisoners for personal gain

(What can I say? Not one drop of blood was spilt at Geelong. People out of the goodness of their hearts, offer you gifts and you should hurt their feelings by rebuffing them? Surely not. When the Queen goes for a walk to stretch her royal legs people give her flowers. When she has a birthday the king of Bongo Congo sends her an umbrella stand made from an elephant's foot and no one gives a stuff. They didn't send the old dear back to Pentridge for copping the occasional sling.) December 28, 1984

Released from jail in November 1986

File Notes: 25 November 1986

Mark Read

Read attended this evening at 6 pm as required. He instantly recognised a large potential problem in another pre-releasee. Apparently Read was involved in an incident in prison in 1975 where the other man was hit with a baseball bat, and there has been ill-feeling between the groups ever since.

Both parties reacted significantly this evening, which makes the writer feel there is probably mostly truth in the allegations. It is our

*intention to have Read report to the centre at 1pm this Thursday,
27 November, to 'do' his three hours.*

*At this time a future possible placement will be discussed, as a
psychiatric referral (which has been requested by Read).*

Read left the centre (with permission) at 7.30pm.
Gerry O'Donnell

Read recalls:

In November 1986 I was released from Bendigo prison and
ordered to report to the pre-release attendance centre in
Carlton, it was situated near Lygon Street, in fact, it could be
seen clearly from the Bowling Green Hotel, where Dennis
Allen sometimes drank while waiting for his mother, who
also had to report there. When I went in, she saw me and ran
screaming into the office ranting and raving about how I had
bashed her young son Dennis over his pinhead with a baseball
bat. Actually, I did him a favour, because he had a head which
needed regular panel beating.

There was some other non-event, two bob gangster
there as well, who joined in on the baseball bat story, and
complained that I'd hit him with a baseball bat as well.
Who did these characters think I was, Babe Ruth?

I told the people in charge that this was total nonsense.

I had in fact hit Allen over the head nine times with a large
rolling pin. I thought he 'kneaded' it, ha ha.

As for the other numbskull, I hit him with a mop
bucket, there was never a baseball bat in sight. Nevertheless,

they refused to accept me at the attendance centre. All in all, they sent me to two more attendance centres, but it was the same old story. Every time I would walk in, some crim would run to the office and sob out a story about how I had allegedly flogged him inside. In the end, they told me not to come in and just to check in via the phone. The Parole Board ended up sending me to Tasmania as it was easier for all concerned.

My popularity or lack of it in criminal circles was always a problem for the Parole Board. I was as popular as a hand grenade in a wedding cake. Bugger it, popularity has never been the aim of the game in my mind.

Mark Brandon Read
Unit 11/ No 1, Blyth St
Ravenswood, Launceston
Tasmania 7250

Hello Mr Jeffery,
It is I, Chopper, alive and well in the rural splendour of Tasmania. I'm on the Dole, I've got a bank account with the Launceston Bank of Savings.

Dad introduced me to the police within half an hour of me getting off the plane. My sins in the mainland mean nothing in their eyes down here.

If anyone farts in my general direction, from a distance of 300 yards, they are in bother. Ha ha.

Thank you for your help and understanding in this matter.

Maybe one day, I may be able to do you a kindness. What more
can I say apart from take care and thank you once again.

Regards,
Mark Brandon Read.

After Read was released from jail on 24 November 1986, he
claimed to be finished with crime and living quietly in
Tasmania. But retirement was not for him; he secretly returned
to Melbourne for hit run raids on drug dealers. In the early
hours of 12 June 1987, Read went to the Bojangles Nightclub
and shot dead 'Sammy the Turk', Siam Ozerkam. Read was
charged with murder. But, while he never denied shooting
Ozerkam in the left eye with a shotgun at point blank range,
he claimed it was self defence. In the end, to his surprise, the
jury believed him and he was acquitted of murder.

Mark Brandon Read
H Div
PO Box 114
Coburg, Vic, 3058

Dear Mr Jeffery,
I received a couple of notices from the parole people — orders for the
cancellation of my pre-release permit. Is this a normal state of
affairs? And how does this leave me?
  Should I be granted bail or found not guilty at court, what the
hell did you tell them in your report?

If I am granted bail can anything be done? A bribe is not totally out of the question. If I am found not guilty, where do I stand? I hope this does not mean my parole is cancelled.

My God, all this fuss over a wog. Murder should be a five bob fine. Murder is too strong a word in this instance. I guess one could explain it away as Anglo-Turkish relations gone wrong.

I'd rather be tried by 12 than carried by six. Surely the Parole Board can wait to flex their biceps 'till after I'm found guilty, and that hasn't happened yet. God is a Mason and a white man and he will protect me.

Let me know what's going on.

Thank you,
Mark Brandon Read Esq.

29 July 1987

To Mr Mark Read,
H Division, Pentridge

Dear Mark,
In answer to your question regarding pre-release. It is the practice of the Parole Board to cancel a pre-release permit when the conditions of the permit cannot be complied with. In your case you are in custody and cannot comply with the conditions. Should you be given bail the board does have the power to then release you on pre-release, but looking at the charge you are now facing I do not believe the board would release you.

Should you be found not guilty or the matter is withdrawn by the Crown, the board would look at your case. The board has the power to keep you inside or release you, that is up to the board. I would think that the chances of being released are good, but that is only my opinion.

Mark, a bribe is totally out of the question. I am not prepared to comment on your comments about Anglo-Turkish relations, or if God is a Mason.

Yours Sincerely,
Jim Jeffery,
Acting Assistant Regional Manager,
Northcote Community Corrections Centre

CHAPTER 6

CHOPPER'S RULES
OF SURVIVAL

IF CAUGHT IN A ROBBERY

Do not look the gunman in the eye.

Do not look physically threatening.

Do not get caught between gunman and money or gunman and the exit.

Compare gunman to an object. They always look bigger when carrying a gun.

Give up your wallet or purse. Money can be replaced. A pancreas can't.

Listen. Gunmen can disguise their looks but rarely their voices.

Look at the way they walk. That doesn't change.

Don't take it too seriously. It'll be a story to tell your grandchildren.

IF CAUGHT IN A RIP

Immediately remove knuckledusters, knives, iron bars and guns from board-shorts. It is hard to swim when carrying ten kilos of hardware.

IF ABDUCTED BY A HITMAN

Don't beg. Offer money. You already know he can be bought for a price. Many people have come back from the edge of their grave because they kept their wits about them and their wallets open. Don't show him pictures of your kids. Show him pictures of your bank manager.

Never play the gangster. Someone might take you seriously.

Never fight someone whose name ends in a Vic of Ich. Likewise if their family name comes before their given name.

Never fight a man whose nickname is Mad or Chopper.

Never trust a friend. The cemeteries are full of people who did.

Never trust a tradesman.

Never trust a Frenchman.

Never fight a policeman from the Special Operations Group unless you like eating your food through a straw.

Never tease a fool.

Never fight an Eskimo.

Never pick on old men in brown suits. They are probably ex-detectives.

Always give way to women under thirty driving Korean cars. They are the modern Kamikazes.

Never get involved in road rage: Men will fight to the death over a scratch to their second-hand Commodores but do nothing when their wives are raped by bikies. Go figure.

Never eat steamed dim sims. I know the names of at least seven crooks who have ended up a Chinese mincer.

Never eat a battered savaloy. Ditto.

Never eat anything described as 'surprise' – whether seafood surprise, chicken surprise or anything else. Surprise in restaurant-speak means off.

Never send food back to the kitchen. A chef told me he has a wall of pictures where the steaks have been placed between the cheeks of the apprentice's bottom before being returned to smart-arse dinners.

If you walk into a bar and can't recognise the music – leave immediately.

If the barmaid is beautiful, leave. The drinks will be inflated in direct relation to her bra size.

If the barman looks like a bodybuilder and has tattoos – leave. You have walked into a gay bar.

Never start what you can't finish. Food, fights, books, long-distance swims and, as the Morans found out, underworld wars.

Never buy your wife crotchless panties for Valentine's Day. For some reason they don't find them romantic.

Never marry your mistress. She already knows you're a cheater.

Never go unarmed to a women's shoe sale.

Never use a power tool in the bath.

Never own a cat.

Never argue about sport. You can't change the result but you can end up in jail after the punch-on.

Know when to retire gracefully. (Too late for you, Alphonse.)

Never buy a book that has Judy Moran on the cover.

Never stand between Judy and an all-you-can-eat buffet. You will wake up in hospital.

Never go to a psychiatrist. They are all mad.

Never go to a social worker. They all need help.

Lawyers near money are like puppies near slippers. Neither can help themselves. Leave a lawyer near money and he'll end up with it all. Leave a puppy near slippers and he'll chew them into little pieces. They can't help it. The lesson is to keep the money and the slippers out of harm's way.

A bad story is better than no story.

Never walk into a small back room in a Carlton restaurant with Mick Gatto to pick a fight.

Never plead guilty.

Thank God for juries.

Now you can buy any of these other *Chopper* books by Mark Brandon Read from your bookshop or direct from his publisher.

Free P+P and UK Delivery (Abroad £3.00 per book)

Chopper
ISBN 978-1-84454-349-6   PB   £6.99

Chopper 2 – How to Shoot Friends and Influence People
ISBN 978-1-84454-382-3   PB   £6.99

Chopper 3 – Hell Hath No Fury Like a Mate Shot in the Arse
ISBN 978-1-84454-040-2   PB   £6.99

Chopper 4 – Happiness is a Warm Gun
ISBN 978-1-84454-094-5   PB   £7.99

Chopper 5 – Don't Go Breaking My Legs
ISBN 978-184454-269-7   PB   £7.99

Chopper 6 – A Bullet in Time Saves Nine
ISBN 978-1-84454-502-5   PB   £7.99

Chopper 7 – Gentlemen Prefer Guns
ISBN 978-1-84454-355-7   PB   £7.99

Chopper 8 – A Bullet in the Head is Worth Two in the Chamber
ISBN 978-1-84454-5353   HB   £17.99

Chopper 9 – Some Don't Like It Hot
ISBN 978-1-84454-647-3   HB   £17.99

TO ORDER SIMPLY CALL THIS NUMBER
+ 44 (0) 207 381 0666

Or visit our website www.johnblakepublishing.co.uk
Prices and availability subject to change without notice